Vegan Feasts

Rose Elliot is Britain's foremost vegetarian cookery writer and her books have won her popular acclaim in all parts of the English-speaking world.

Rose has been in the vanguard of the revolution in our eating habits in recent years, as more and more people consume less meat and take greater interest in healthy eating. She frequently contributes to magazines, gives cookery demonstrations and broadcasts on radio and television. Rose is also a professional astrologer and, with her husband, runs a computer-based astrological service which provides personality profiles, forecasts and compatibility charts. (For more details, please send SAE to Rose Elliot, PO Box 16, Eastleigh SO5 6BH, UK.)

Other Thorsons books by Rose Elliot

Vegetarian Christmas
The Bean Book
Cheap and Easy
Low Fat, Low Sugar

Vegan
Feasts

ROSE ELLIOT

Thorsons

Thorsons
An Imprint of HarperCollins*Publishers*
77-85 Fulham Palace Road,
Hammersmith, London W6 8JB

The Thorsons website address is www.thorsons.com

First published by Thorsons 1997
This edition published 2000

10 9 8 7 6 5 4 3 2 1

Text illustrations by Helen Holroyd

A catalogue record for this book
is available from the British Library

ISBN 0 7225 4006 X

Printed and bound in Great Britain by
Martins the Printers Limited, Berwick upon Tweed

contents

introduction

I have particularly enjoyed writing this book of vegan – or dairy-free vegetarian – recipes. When I first started writing about vegetarian cookery, part of the pleasure for me lay in the challenge of creating delicious dishes from a limited range of ingredients, and in people's surprise when they realized how good they could be.

In many ways, being a vegan today feels similar to how it felt being vegetarian when I began my career. Now, though, vegetarianism is pretty mainstream – eating out, buying ingredients or ready-made meals are all relatively easy, and friends and acquaintances no longer recoil in dismay at the thought of having to cook for a vegetarian. Vegans today, however, have much the same difficulties vegetarians used to have. Packets in shops have to be scrutinized carefully – whey seems to be in almost everything; the choice when eating out or buying prepared foods is often limited and, yes, you've guessed it, friends find it difficult to know what to cook, exclaiming, "Well what on earth *do* you eat, then?" They worry, too, about whether or not malnutrition has set in, perhaps destroying a few brain cells along the way.

Poet Benjamin Zephaniah explains what vegans eat more eloquently than I ever could in his rap poem "Vegan Delight" on page vii – my warmest thanks to him for allowing me to include it. This book gives around 160 recipes and variations for creating some of the dishes he mentions and others which I have found to be easy to make and good to eat. And on pages x–xiii, I've suggested some vegan menus to give you a few ideas for combining the recipes. Regarding the nutritional aspect of a vegan diet, I have discussed the main issues of concern on pages viii–x, and I am indebted to Dr Michael Klaper for permission to use his nutrition chart. Follow this and you'll eat well and feel fit and full of vitality.

Vegan Delight

by Benjamin Zephaniah

Ackees, chapattis
Dumplins an nan,
Channa an rotis
Onion uttapam,
Masala dosa
Green callaloo
Bhel an samosa
Corn an aloo.
Yam an cassava
Pepperpot stew,
Rotlo an guava
Rice an tofu,
Puri, paratha
Sesame casserole,
Brown eggless pasta
An brown bread rolls.

Soya milked muesli
Soya bean curd,
Soya sweet sweeties
Soya's de word,
Soya bean margarine
Soya bean sauce,
What can mek medicine?
Soya of course.
Soya meks yogurt

Soya ice-cream,
Or soya sorbert
Soya reigns supreme,
Soya sticks liquoriced
Soya salads
Try any soya dish
Soya is bad.

Plantain an tabouli
Cornmeal pudding
Onion bhajee
Wid plenty cumin,
Breadfruit an coconuts
Molasses tea
Dairy-free omelettes
Very chilli.
Gingerbread, nut roast
Sorrell, paw paw,
Cocoa an rye toast
I tek dem on tour,
Drinking cool maubi
Meks me feel sweet,
What was dat question now?
What do we eat?

© Benjamin Zephaniah, 1994

eating healthily and well

If you eat according to the suggestions given in this book, you will get all the nutrients you need. The vegan diet is a healthy one, as study after study has shown. Yet, because meat-eating is part of our culture and due to the messages portrayed through advertising by and on behalf of the meat and dairy industries, people still worry that they may be lacking in nutrients if they follow a vegetarian diet, and even more so if they follow a vegan one. The nutrients most vegetarians and vegans are concerned they may not be getting enough of are protein, iron, calcium and vitamin B_{12}, so I will comment briefly on these.

Protein

Protein is the nutrient most people mention first when they ask about whether or not a vegetarian or vegan diet is healthy, but, really, there is no problem with getting enough protein with either kind of diet. Grains, pulses (legumes), soya milk, nuts and even potatoes all contain protein and the amounts add up during the course of a day, so protein deficiency is extremely rare in the affluent countries of the world. Additionally, nutritionists often say that vegetarians and vegans have to mix, combine or balance proteins of different types in order to get the correct number of amino acids. This is not correct. In 1993, the authoritative and respected American Dietetic Association stated: "Plant sources of protein alone can provide adequate amounts of the essential and non-essential amino acids, assuming that dietary protein sources from plants are reasonably varied and that calorie intake is sufficient to meet energy needs. Whole grains, legumes, vegetables, seeds and nuts all contain essential and non-essential amino acids. Conscious combining of these foods within a given meal, as the complementary protein dictum suggests, is unnecessary. Additionally, soya protein has been shown to be nutritionally equivalent in protein value to proteins of animal origin and, thus, can serve as the sole source of protein intake if desired."

Iron

Iron deficiency is one of the most common problems in the Western diet, but what is often overlooked by doctors and others is that scientific studies have shown that vegetarians and vegans are no more likely to suffer from this than meat-eaters. In fact, research has shown their iron intake to be as high or higher than that of meat-eaters. A study of British vegans in 1978 found the iron level "normal in all the vegans and no subject had a haemoglobin concentration below the lower limit of normality".[1] Another study in 1985 found the dietary intakes of vegans to be more than double the official estimated average requirement[2] and yet another in Israel in 1986 compared the iron intakes of meat-eaters and vegetarians and found that "the intake of iron was significantly higher in vegetarians… it concluded that a long-term ovo-lacto vegetarian diet does not lead to mineral deficiencies".[3] This has been found to be so in children, too. A study in Holland which compared meat-eating and vegetarian pre-school children found that while the vegetarian children had a good intake of dietary iron, the meat-eaters "had intakes of iron below the Dutch recommended daily allowances".[4]

Calcium

Although vegans don't eat what are conventionally considered to be the best sources of calcium – cow's milk and cheese – there isn't evidence of calcium deficiency. In fact, what is not generally known is that these dairy products are not very helpful because although they do contain plenty of calcium, they also contain a great deal of protein. It appears that too much acid is produced when these are digested, which means that the body needs to neutralize it by releasing calcium from the bones before it is excreted in the urine. So, the calcium from such sources is badly absorbed and, in fact, causes more to be lost, as is suggested by the findings that the Eskimos have one of the highest calcium intakes in the world but also one of the highest incidences of osteoporosis.[5]

Although vegans and vegetarians may consume less calcium than meat-eaters, their bodies seem to use and store it far more efficiently than meat-eaters. This is thought to be because of the quantities of boron present in vegan and vegetarian diets. Boron is a trace element found in apples, pears, pulses (legumes), leafy vegetables and nuts. There is none in dairy produce or meat. Many of the foods which contain boron are also often rich in calcium. A cupful of broccoli, for instance, contains as much calcium as 200ml (6fl oz) of cow's milk, and sesame seeds, tahini, hummus, tofu, soya milk, almonds and dark green leafy vegetables are further rich sources.

Vitamin B_{12}

This vitamin is essential for the development of blood cells and the healthy functioning of the nervous system, so we need to be sure that we get enough of it. However, unlike many vitamins, B_{12} can be stored by the body, so it's not one you need to have every day. Also, you only need minuscule amounts – the equivalent of one millionth of a gram per day.

Vegetarians and vegans can easily ensure adequate intakes of this vitamin by eating the many foods fortified with B_{12}, such as yeast extracts, yeast-based spreads and pâtés, most breakfast cereals, soya milk and textured vegetable proteins. Read the packets to see if the vitamin is listed in the ingredients.

If you are really worried and unsure whether or not you are getting enough B_{12}, you can always take a B vitamin complex supplement, but this is unlikely to be necessary if you are eating a varied, healthy range of foods.

What can we conclude from this?

Nutritionally, vegetarian and vegan diets are not problematical and there are, in fact, numerous health benefits. It is weird that although every health study undertaken points to the positive health benefits of a vegetarian or vegan diet (and the disadvantages of animal fats and proteins), people still worry that in becoming vegetarian or vegan we may be risking our health! The evidence points to exactly the opposite. For instance, the Oxford Vegetarian Study – an ongoing study of 6,000 vegetarians and 5,000 meat-eaters over 12 years – examined the likelihood of dying from cancer or heart disease. The interim results, reported on 25 June 1994, show that vegetarians and vegans have a 40 per cent reduced risk of dying from cancer, a 30 per cent reduced risk of heart disease and a 20 per cent reduced risk of premature mortality from all other causes. Another piece of research has shown that vegans and vegetarians are five times less likely to be admitted to hospital than meat-eaters. Indeed, numerous other studies have come up with similar findings that there are huge health benefits to be gained by becoming vegetarian and then taking the next logical step and becoming vegan. Apart from the personal benefits, such a move has a positive impact on world ecology and reduces animal suffering.

It is vital you eat a varied balanced diet for good health. Breakfast is a good time to try some of the many grains, perhaps in the form of a bowl of oats and other flaked grains (such as rye, wheat or barley) with raisins or chopped dried apricots, maybe a few chopped or grated nuts and soya milk, which counts as one serving of pulses (legumes). Another good breakfast is porridge made with half soya milk and half water, topped with some flaked almonds or hazelnuts and perhaps a few raisins or some maple syrup for sweetness. Or, for a lighter breakfast, soya yogurt and fresh fruit make for a good start to the day. All these suggestions can be rounded off with wholewheat toast, vegan margarine and any preserves you fancy, as well as tea, coffee, herb tea or whatever you like to drink at breakfast.

There are plenty of possibilities for quick snack meals, too. Almost any of the dips in this book can be whizzed up in no time and if you haven't got time even for that, then hummus is widely available and good on toast, bread or pitta bread or in sandwiches with some salad. A burger in a bun – especially the Spicy Beanburgers on page 99 makes a good quick snack and they can be cooked from frozen. Refried Red Beans on page 105 are very quick to prepare if you use canned beans, or if you have a supply of cooked beans in the freezer, and these are delicious jazzed up with sliced avocado, tortilla chips, tomato and other salad ingredients. Red Bean Chilli on page 107 is speedy to cook and makes a filling meal, especially if served with a baked potato. Talking of baked potatoes, to the question "What can I have with it instead of cheese?", there are plenty of answers on page 134. Some of my favourites are coleslaw, mashed avocado, chopped fresh herbs and vegan margarine, lemon and fresh herb sauce, tahini dressing, hummus or bean pâté – and there are many other possibilities.

Pasta, of course, makes a good, quick, pleasurable meal that most people like. For a whole host of good vegan sauces, see pages 80–95. If you want an extra topping in place of Parmesan, try chopped fresh herbs, pine nuts or even a scattering of crunchy croutons, all of which work well. Particular favourites of mine are Penne with Artichoke Hearts, Sun-dried Tomatoes, Olives and Basil, Fusilli Colbucco with Aubergine (Eggplant) and Wine Sauce and Lasagne al Forno (pages 80–94).

Potato-based dishes are good for quick meals, so try Rosti, Colcannon, Champ, Healthy Chips (Fries) and Potato Pancakes (pages 133–143), which are all excellent in this respect. To turn them into well-balanced, healthy meals, simply serve them with a good salad, perhaps including grated carrot, sliced tomatoes and green leaves.

Pastry dishes make excellent main courses and are particularly useful as the centrepiece of a special meal. Spanikopita (page 70) is wonderful in the summer, served with just a ripe tomato and basil salad, with perhaps an asparagus vinaigrette as an appetizer and Instant Raspberry Ice for pudding. Flaky Potato Pie is another great dish for a special meal, while Chestnut and Red Wine Pâté, Flaky Mushroom Roll or Ann's Pie (pages 56–79) all make popular main courses for Christmas, although I still think there's a place for a really good Nut Roast (pages 130–1). All of these need to be served with complementary sauces, and there are a number of tasty possibilities in the section starting on page 42.

I especially enjoyed working on the Desserts and Cakes and Cookies chapters in this book. It was very satisfying to create really good vegan versions of favourites such as Raspberry Ice, Kulfi – that delectable, fragrant Indian ice – Chocolate Mousse, Chocolate Torte and Steamed Syrup Pudding, not to mention the superb Fruit Cake, amazingly light and tasty Sponge Cake, with several variations, and the very good Sticky Date Ginger Cake (page 144–171). In fact, the results were so good that I began to wonder why we generally use eggs in these recipes at all! I hope you will enjoy them, and all the other recipes in this book, too.

A note on ingredients and measures

Nearly all the ingredients you need for vegan cookery are easy to find. Read the labels; you will soon get to know which products are suitable and find your favourites.

SOYA MILKS, MARGARINES AND CREAM

There are numerous soya milks and vegan margarines and you really need to just try them all out to find which ones are your favourites. Of the margarines, I particularly like an unsalted one made with cold-pressed oils available from healthfood shops. Vegan cream, made from soya, is also available. Again, it is a case of trying the different brands to see which one you like best. There is an excellent one flavoured delicately with real vanilla.

OILS

My preference is for olive oil, except for deep or shallow frying, for which I think a chemically stable oil such as rape or soya is best. When frying onion, garlic or other such ingredient at the beginning of a recipe, I use a little olive oil. This can be a blended

How to meet daily nutritional requirements on a vegan diet

Food group	How often to eat	What it provides	Some examples
whole grains and potatoes	2–4 100g (4oz) servings daily	energy, protein, oils, vitamins, fibre	brown rice, corn, millet, barley, bulgur, buckwheat, oats, muesli, bread, pasta, flour
pulses (legumes)	1–2 100g (4oz) servings daily	protein, oils	green peas, lentils, chickpeas (garbanzos), kidney beans, baked beans, soya products
green and yellow vegetables	1–3 100g (4oz) servings daily	vitamins, minerals, protein	broccoli, Brussels sprouts, spinach, cabbage, carrots, marrow, sweet potatoes, pumpkins, parsnips
nuts and seeds	1–3 25g (1oz) servings daily	energy, protein, oils, calcium, trace minerals	almonds, pumpkin seeds, walnuts, peanuts, sesame seeds, nut butters, tahini, sunflower seeds
fruit	3–6 pieces daily	energy, vitamins, minerals	all kinds
vitamin and mineral foods	1 serving of (a) and (b) 3 times a week	trace minerals and vitamin B_{12}	(a) sea vegetables (b) B_{12}-fortified foods, such as soya milk, TVP and breakfast cereals

Based on a table by Dr Michael Klaper,

used with his kind permission

olive oil – the cheapest – saving the best you can afford for dressing and finishing a dish, where the flavour and colour really count.

HERBS AND SPICES

Herbs and spices really give flavour to vegan dishes. My advice is to gradually build up a collection of your favourite spices. Some herbs dry well and are useful to keep on hand, such as bay leaves, oregano, thyme and rosemary. Others are far better fresh and it's great that they are so easy to get now.

SALT

While writing this book, I've become more aware of the health risks relating to salt, or perhaps I should put it another way – the health benefits of reducing your intake of salt. Studies have shown that a reduction in salt intake has the positive effect of lowering raised blood pressure, which in turn means a lower risk of heart attacks and stroke. The campaign in Finland to reduce the population's intake of salt over the last 12 years or so has resulted in a reduction in the incidence of high blood pressure and a remarkable decrease in cases of both stroke and coronary heart disease.

Having found this out, one of my previous "vices" – my liking for salt – is being disciplined and I've replaced my favourite sea salt with a low-sodium "salt" available from supermarkets. Of course, the ideal is to become familiar with the clear, fresh flavour of foods prepared with the minimum of salt or none at all, and this I am working on. The amount of salt you add to recipes and the type is, of course, up to you, but I do believe it's something worth considering. Perhaps we can take comfort in also noting the increasing evidence that drinking wine, in moderation, has positive health benefits and enjoy our fresh-tasting vegan meals with a glass of our favourite wine. Cheers!

MEASURES

In the recipes, the measures are given in metric, imperial and American cups. For the best results, stick to one system of measurement throughout a recipe and measure carefully – especially the first time you make a recipe and where this is important, such as for pastry. After that, feel free to make the recipe your own and be creative by adding other ingredients, herbs and so on as you wish. Bon appétit!

Footnotes

1) T. A. Sanders, F. R. Ellis, J. W. Dickerson, 'Haematological studies on vegans', *British Journal of Nutrition,* July 1978, 40 (1), pp. 9–15

2) E. Carlson, M. Kipps, A. Lockie, J. J. Thompson, 'A comparative evaluation of vegan, vegetarian and omnivore diets', *Plant Foods,* 6 (1985), pp. 89–100

3) N. Levin, J. Rattan, T. Gilat, 'Mineral and blood levels in vegetarians', *Israeli Journal of Medical Science,* February 1986, 22 (2), pp. 105–8

4) W. A. van Staveron, J. H. Dhuyvetter, A. Bons, M. Zeelen, J. G. Hautvast, 'Food consumption and height/weight status of Dutch preschool children on alternative diets', *Journal of the American Diet Association,* December 1985, 85 (12), pp. 1579–84

5) R. B. Mazess, 'Bone mineral content of North Alaskan Eskimos', *The American Journal of Clinical Nutrition,* 1974, 27, (9), pp. 916–25

soups

These light and refreshing soups make perfect appetizers, and can be served either hot or chilled. The recipes are very easy to make – no complicated techniques are involved and no hours of stock-making – yet the results are still delicious. If you want a smooth soup, it helps to have a liquidizer or food processor, but many of the soups are equally good served unliquidized.

It's possible to make a good vegan stock by simmering an onion, carrot, a few celery sticks, a bay leaf, sprig of thyme and some parsley stalks in plenty of water for a couple of hours, then strain it and discard the vegetables and herbs. However, I rarely do this. Occasionally I might buy a really good-quality vegetable bouillon powder, available from healthfood shops, but I prefer to use water which allows the pure and unadulterated flavours of the vegetables to stand out. Try these soups and see what I mean.

green pea and mint soup

This soup is refreshing and quick to make, and is equally good served hot or chilled. If possible, use frozen petits pois or baby peas for their delicious sweet flavour.

serves 4

1 onion, chopped
1tbsp olive oil
225g/8oz/1^1/2 cups potatoes, peeled and cut into 1cm/^{1}/2in dice
450g/1lb/3^1/4 cups frozen petits pois (baby peas)
4–5 sprigs of mint
900ml/1^1/2 pints/3^3/4 cups water or light vegetable stock
1–2tbsp freshly squeezed lemon juice
sea salt
freshly ground black pepper
soya cream, optional, to serve
chopped fresh mint, to garnish

Heat the oil in a large saucepan. Add the onion and fry, without browning, for 5 minutes. Add the potatoes, stir well, cover, and continue to cook it gently, taking care not to brown the vegetables, for a further 5–10 minutes. Add the peas, mint and water or stock, then bring to the boil, cover, and simmer for 15–20 minutes, until the vegetables are very tender.

Purée the soup in a blender or food processor, then transfer it to a clean saucepan. If you want a very smooth texture, pour it through a sieve into the pan. Adjust the consistency with extra water, if necessary. Add the lemon juice and season with salt and pepper to taste. Reheat, and serve with a spoonful of soya cream, if using, and a sprinkling of chopped fresh mint.

creamy potato and onion soup

This creamy soup is thickened entirely with puréed potato, which gives it a soothing and satisfying consistency.

serves 4–6

Put a quarter of the onions into a large saucepan with the potatoes and water. Bring to the boil, then cover, and cook for 15–20 minutes, until the potatoes are tender. Meanwhile, heat the margarine and oil in another pan. Add the remaining onions and cook them over a low heat, covered, for about 15 minutes, until they are very tender. Don't let them brown.

   Purée the potato mixture in a blender or food processor, then return it to the saucepan. Add the onions and salt, pepper and grated nutmeg to taste. Reheat gently and serve.

4 onions, sliced
450g/1lb/3 cups potatoes, peeled and cut into even-sized chunks
1 litre/1³/₄ pints/4¹/₃ cups water
40g/1¹/₂oz/3tbsp vegan margarine
1tbsp olive oil
salt
freshly ground black pepper
freshly grated nutmeg

tomato soup

This popular soup is very quick and easy to make.

serves 4

1tbsp olive oil
1 onion, chopped
350g/12oz/2^1/$_2$ cups potatoes, peeled and diced
450g/1lb/3 cups tomatoes, skinned and sliced, or
425g/15oz can tomatoes
900ml/1^1/$_2$ pints/3^3/$_4$ cups water
salt
freshly ground black pepper

Heat the olive oil in a large saucepan. Add the onion and cook, covered, without browning, for 5 minutes. Add the potatoes, cover again, and cook gently for a further 5–10 minutes.

Add the tomatoes and cook, stirring occasionally, for a further 4–5 minutes but do not allow the vegetables to brown. Add the water, cover, and leave the soup to simmer for 15–20 minutes, until the potatoes are tender.

Purée the soup in a blender or food processor until smooth. If you want a really smooth soup, it can then be strained to remove the tomato seeds, although this isn't essential. Season with salt and pepper to taste, and reheat gently, without boiling, before serving.

watercress soup

serves 4

Heat the olive oil in a large saucepan. Add the onion and cook, covered, without browning, for 5 minutes.

Add the potatoes, cover, and cook gently for a further 5–10 minutes. Stir from time to time and do not allow the vegetables to brown. Add the water then leave the soup to simmer for about 20 minutes, until the potatoes are tender.

Purée the soup and watercress in a blender or food processor. Season with salt and pepper to taste, then reheat gently before serving.

1tbsp olive oil
1 onion, chopped
700g/1½lb/4½ cups potatoes, peeled and diced
900ml/1½ pints/3¾ cups water
1 bunch of watercress
salt
freshly ground black pepper

carrot and ginger soup

A delicately flavoured soup with a beautiful colour.

serves 4

2tbsp olive oil
1 onion, chopped
450g/1lb/3^{1}/4 cups carrots, scraped and sliced
225g/8oz/1^{1}/2 cups potatoes, peeled and diced
1tsp grated fresh root ginger
salt
900ml/1^{1}/2 pints/3^{3}/4 cups water
freshly ground black pepper

Heat the olive oil in a large saucepan. Add the onion and cook gently for 5 minutes. Add the carrots, potatoes, ginger and a pinch of salt and fry, covered, for a further 10 minutes, stirring from time to time. Add the water, bring to the boil, then simmer for about 15 minutes, until the carrots are tender.

Purée the soup in a blender or food processor, then thin with a little extra water, if necessary. Return the soup to the cleaned saucepan, then season with salt and pepper.

variation

carrot, lime and coriander (cilantro) soup

Follow the method, above, but replace the ginger with the zest of 1 lime, cut into long strips (if you do not have a zester, finely grate the zest). Flavour the puréed soup with the juice of the lime, adding it gradually and tasting until it is to your liking. Garnish with 2–3 tablespoons of chopped fresh coriander (cilantro) leaves, 1 teaspoon of coarsely crushed coriander seeds and the lime zest.

leek and potato soup

Heat the oil in a large saucepan. Add the leeks and potatoes and cook gently, covered, without browning, for 20 minutes. Stir the vegetables often to prevent them sticking to the pan.

Add the water, stir, then simmer for 5–10 minutes, until the vegetables are tender.

Purée in a blender or food processor. Season with salt and pepper to taste, stir, and serve in warmed bowls, sprinkled with chopped parsley, if using.

2tbsp olive oil

3 leeks, sliced

700g/1^1/2lb/4^1/2 cups potatoes, peeled and diced

1 litre/1^3/4 pints/4^1/3 cups water

chopped fresh parsley, to garnish, optional

sweet red pepper soup with basil

Peppers make a smooth, sweet soup, which is good served either hot or cold.

serves 4

1 onion, chopped

1tbsp olive oil

4 sweet yellow peppers, seeded and cut into 1cm/^{1}/$_2$in dice

2 garlic cloves, crushed (minced)

225g/8oz/1^1/$_2$ cups potatoes, peeled and cut into 1cm/^{1}/$_2$in dice

900ml/1^1/$_2$ pints/3^3/$_4$ cups water or light vegetable stock

salt

freshly ground black pepper

juice of ^{1}/$_2$ lemon

sprigs of fresh basil, optional, to garnish

black peppercorns, coarsely crushed, to garnish, optional

Heat the oil in a large saucepan. Add the onion and cook, without browning, for 5 minutes. Add the peppers, garlic and potatoes. Stir well, then cover, and continue to cook gently for a further 5–10 minutes, taking care not to brown the vegetables.

Add the water or stock, bring to the boil, cover, and simmer for 15–20 minutes, until the vegetables are very tender.

Purée the soup in a blender or food processor and return it to the cleaned pan, adjusting the consistency with extra water, if necessary. Reheat the soup and add the lemon juice, a tablespoonful at a time until it is how you like it. Season with salt and pepper to taste. Serve garnished with a sprig of basil and a sprinkling of crushed peppercorns, if using.

tuscan bean soup

This soup makes a perfect light meal when served on its own with bread. Alternatively, serve it with assorted crostini and a salad for a more substantial meal. The quantities given are for two people, but you can easily serve a couple of friends too, by doubling the amount of beans and water.

serves 2

If using dried beans, soak and cook as described on page 97. Drain and reserve 150ml/5fl oz/generous $^1/_2$ cup of the cooking liquid.

Heat the oil in a large saucepan. Add the onion, cover, and cook gently, without browning, for 10 minutes, until the onion is tender. Add the garlic and cook for 1–2 minutes. Add the cannellini beans, together with the reserved soaking liquid or water, then stir. Purée in a food processor or blender until fairly smooth and creamy. Return the mixture to the pan with about 300ml/ 10fl oz/1$^1/_4$ cups of water. This will make a medium-thick soup, but you can add more or less water, if liked. Bring the soup to the boil, then season with salt, pepper and a squeeze or two of lemon juice.

Serve the soup in warmed bowls, drizzled with olive oil and a sprinkling of parsley, if using, and some coarsely ground black pepper.

1tbsp extra virgin olive oil, plus extra to serve, optional
1 onion, chopped
2 garlic cloves, crushed (minced)
425g/15oz can cannellini beans, drained, or
100g/3$^1/_2$oz/$^1/_2$ cup dried cannellini beans
salt
freshly ground black pepper
fresh lemon juice
handful of flat-leaf parsley, coarsely chopped, to garnish, optional

Dips are particularly useful for vegans because they are a good alternative to cheese, cream cheese or soured cream as a topping for dishes like baked potatoes and salads. Dips also make brilliant quick snacks; serve them with potato or tortilla chips, various breads, including toast and crostini, and, of course, fresh vegetables. In addition to their versatility, they can also be extremely nutritious.

crudités

This colourful assortment of vegetables is ideal for serving with dips, either as part of a light, pre-meal nibble or as a snack at any other time of the day. They also make nutritious snacks for children.

Choose really fresh, crisp vegetables in contrasting colours and with varying flavours. Have at least three different types of vegetable, arranged in little heaps on a lettuce leaf-lined plate or tray, or alternatively pile them up in a small basket with the dips arranged around the outside.

Try:

- radishes, with the roots trimmed but the leaves left on
- spring onions (scallions), trimmed
- julienne of carrots
- crisp celery sticks
- slices of sweet red, green or yellow pepper
- batons of cucumber
- cauliflower or broccoli florets
- crisp chicory (endive) leaves – especially good for scooping up dips
- large, juicy black olives
- cherry tomatoes
- baby button mushrooms
- mangetout peas, topped and tailed.

easy bean and herb pâté

You can make this pâté with various canned beans, ranging from earthy brown ful medames (found in Middle Eastern shops), to red kidney beans, white butter beans (lima beans) and cannellini beans, varying the herbs and flavourings to suit the type of bean. It makes a delicious quick dip, or topping for toast, crackers or baked potatoes, or heated through and served as part of a main course with vegetables and rice or pasta.

serves 2

425g/15oz can beans, drained, or 100g/3^{1}/2oz/^{1}/2 cup dried beans, such as cannellini, butter or lima beans, red kidney, ful medames, or your own choice
1 clove garlic, crushed (minced)
2–3tbsp lemon juice
pinch of chilli powder or cayenne
salt
freshly ground black pepper
1–2tbsp chopped fresh herbs, such as parsley, coriander (cilantro) or chives
1tbsp olive oil, optional
paprika or crushed black peppercorns, to garnish, optional

If using dried beans, soak and cook them as described on page 97. Drain the beans, reserving about 150ml/5fl oz/ generous ^{1}/2 cup of the cooking liquid. Mash the beans, a few at a time, with a fork, to make a coarse purée (or you can blend them in a food processor if you prefer).

Mix in the garlic, lemon juice, chilli powder or cayenne and season with salt and pepper to taste, then mix in enough of the reserved cooking liquid or water to achieve the consistency you want.

Mix in the herbs. Add the olive oil, or alternatively drizzle it over the top of the pâté or, for a lower-fat dish, leave it out altogether. A sprinkling of paprika or crushed black peppercorns makes an attractive garnish.

hummus

Although you can easily buy good hummus, it is simple to make using a can of chickpeas (garbanzos). Hummus is a great vegan replacement for mayonnaise and makes a delectable, creamy topping on salads and baked potatoes.

serves 4–6

If using dried beans, soak and cook them as described on page 97. Drain the chickpeas (garbanzos), reserving about 150ml/5fl oz/generous 1/2 cup of the cooking liquid. Put the chickpeas (garbanzos) into a blender or food processor with the garlic and blend to a rough purée.

Add the tahini, lemon juice and oil, then blend again to a smooth cream. Check the consistency and add a tablespoonful or so of the reserved cooking liquid or water, if necessary, to achieve a light, creamy consistency.

Season with salt and pepper and blend again. Spoon into a shallow bowl to serve. Alternatively, spread the hummus out on a plate and level it with a knife so that it is about 1cm/1/2in thick. Pour a little olive oil over the top, then sprinkle with paprika and garnish with lemon wedges, olives and fresh coriander (cilantro), if using.

425g/15oz can chickpeas (garbanzos), drained, or 100g/3½oz/½ cup dried cannellini beans
4–5 cloves garlic, chopped
1tbsp light tahini
4tbsp freshly squeezed lemon juice
1tbsp olive oil
salt
freshly ground black pepper
olive oil, paprika, black olives, lemon wedges and/or fresh coriander (cilantro), to garnish, optional

tahini dip

Like hummus, this moreish dip is packed with nutrients and is excellent with salads or as a filling for sandwiches. It can be served as a dressing or dip with raw vegetables or strips of wholewheat pitta bread, or it is equally good diluted and used as a creamy pouring sauce to accompany steamed vegetables.

serves 1–2

2tbsp tahini
1 clove garlic, crushed (minced)
juice of $\frac{1}{2}$ lemon
salt
freshly ground black pepper

Put the tahini into a small bowl with the garlic, 1 teaspoonful of the lemon juice and 2 tablespoons of water and stir well. The mixture will be very thick and lumpy to start with, then gradually will become smooth and creamy.

Add more water and lemon juice, as necessary, to achieve the desired consistency and flavour, then season with salt and pepper to taste.

guacamole

This authentic Mexican guacamole does not contain lime, or lemon juice but incorporates avocado, tomato, chilli, fresh coriander (cilantro) and seasoning. It is delicious as a dip – served with tortilla chips or fresh vegetables – or as a salad dressing.

serves 3–4

Mash the avocado flesh with a fork, then combine it with the tomatoes, chilli and coriander. Mash and beat the mixture until it has a smooth consistency.

Season with salt and pepper. Spoon into a small bowl and serve immediately since the avocado gradually browns when exposed to the air.

1 large, ripe avocado, stoned and flesh scooped out

2 tomatoes, skinned and finely chopped

$^{1}/_{2}$–1 green chilli, deseeded and finely chopped

$^{1}/_{4}$ bunch fresh coriander (cilantro), finely chopped

salt

freshly ground black pepper

tapenade

This version of the classic Mediterranean dip includes red chilli, garlic and capers. It is excellent with crudités, spread on crackers, or as a topping for baked potatoes.

125g/4oz/1 cup pitted black olives
25g/1oz/¼ cup capers, drained
1 clove garlic, chopped
1 dried chilli, crumbled
4tbsp olive oil
salt
freshly ground black pepper

Put the olives, capers, garlic and chilli into a food processor and whizz until you have a coarse purée. Add the oil and whizz again until blended. Season with salt and pepper to taste. Spoon into a small bowl and serve at room temperature.

sweet red pepper and garlic dip

Put the peppers into a saucepan with the garlic and enough water to just cover them. Bring to the boil, then simmer for about 15 minutes, or until the peppers are very tender. Drain well and leave to cool.

Transfer the peppers and garlic to a food processor and purée. Gradually add the oil and lemon juice until you have a soft, creamy mixture – it should resemble mayonnaise.

Season with salt and pepper to taste, then chill before serving. The dip will thicken slightly as it chills, but you can make it thicker by stirring in some breadcrumbs – add these gradually as they take several minutes to swell.

2 large, sweet red peppers, seeded and quartered

6 large cloves garlic, peeled

150ml/5fl oz/generous $^1/_2$ cup olive oil (not extra-virgin)

1–2tbsp lemon juice

salt

freshly ground black pepper

25–50g/1–2oz/$^1/_2$–1 cup fresh, soft, white bread-crumbs, optional

tofu and sun-dried tomato dip

serves 4

125g/4oz/heaped 1 cup
tofu, drained and cut into
chunks
4 sun-dried tomatoes,
in oil, drained
1 spring onion (scallion),
roughly chopped
1 clove garlic, peeled
salt
freshly ground black pepper

Place the tofu in a food processor or blender with the tomatoes, spring onion (scallion) and garlic. Blend until you have a creamy purée. Season with salt and pepper to taste, and whizz again. Spoon the dip into a small bowl.

variation

tofu, cashew and fresh herb dip

Omit the sun-dried tomatoes and add 75g/3oz/generous $^1/_2$ cup cashew nuts, roasted under the grill (broiler) until golden. Add 1 tablespoon chopped fresh parsley and 1 tablespoon chopped fresh chives and blend.

sandwiches and bread-based snacks

Quick to make, tasty and nourishing, sandwiches and bread-based snacks are as popular with vegans as they are with everyone else, and there are plenty of alternatives to the butter, eggs and cheese often used in fillings and toppings.

Most breads are vegan, but sometimes eggs, butter and other dairy products, such as skimmed milk or buttermilk, are included, so it is best to check the ingredients if you are in doubt.

There are plenty of vegan margarines available, which you can use instead of butter, or you can reduce the calorie and fat content by leaving out the spread. Place the filling straight on to the bread or use some mustard or something similar to add moisture. Many of the dips on pages 10–18 make good fillings and toppings for bread.

sandwiches

Choose your favourite type of bread – light- or heavy-textured wholewheat bread, rye, Granary (Graham) or whatever takes your fancy. Spread it with vegan margarine if you like (you may not need to if the filling is moist), then choose your filling from just some of the many vegan possibilities given below.

If you prefer a toasted sandwich, prepare your chosen filling (see below), spread vegan margarine on 2 pieces of bread, one side only. Spread the filling on the unbuttered side and sandwich the two slices together, enclosing the filling. Toast in a heated sandwich toaster for 4–5 minutes, until crisp and golden brown. Serve immediately.

Vegan sandwich fillings

Here are just a few ideas:

- yeast extract
- yeast extract and wafer-thin cucumber slices or cress
- savoury vegetable pâté
- savoury vegetable pâté and sliced cucumber
- miso
- peanut butter
- peanut butter and sliced cucumber and grated carrot or chopped celery
- peanut butter or tahini and cucumber slices
- Hummus (page 13)
- Hummus (page 13) with a little Tapenade (page 16) or chopped black olives and fresh coriander (cilantro)
- Hummus (page 13) with tomato slices and fresh basil
- Tahini Dip (page 14)
- Tahini Dip with chopped dates or raisins
- Tahini Dip and sprouted mung beans or alfalfa
- Guacamole (page 15)
- Tofu and Sun-dried Tomato Dip (page 18)
- Tofu, Cashew and Fresh Herb Dip (page 18)

- Easy Bean and Herb Pâté (page 12)
- mashed butter beans (lima beans) with chutney
- mashed butter beans (lima beans) and tomato and onion slices
- cucumber, lettuce, tomato, cress, grated carrot
- finely chopped nuts or dates
- mashed cooked red kidney beans with salad
- grated carrot mixed with vinaigrette and chopped herbs or raisins
- vegan cheese, sliced or grated (shredded) with lettuce, tomato, cucumber and vegan mayonnaise
- banana slices with or without peanut butter or sesame spread
- mashed avocado or vegan mayonnaise with cooked asparagus tips or asparagus spears tossed in vinaigrette
- slices of lettuce hearts, avocado slices and chopped walnuts
- shredded lettuce, slices of artichoke hearts, vegan mayonnaise, watercress and toasted pine nuts
- finely sliced mushrooms fried in olive oil with or without garlic, and cooled
- sliced banana and finely grated hazelnuts.

garlic bread

serves 6

1 French stick
3–4 cloves garlic, crushed
(minced)
100ml/3fl oz/scant ½ cup
olive oil

Preheat the oven to 200°C/400°F/Gas 6. Cut deep slices in the French stick, about 2.5cm (1in) apart, making sure the slices are still joined at the base.

Mix the garlic with the oil (or whizz a whole, peeled garlic clove with the olive oil in a blender until the garlic is puréed). Brush the garlic oil over each cut surface of bread. Push the slices together to re-form the loaf, then wrap it in foil or greaseproof paper.

Place the bread on a baking sheet and bake in the preheated oven for about 20 minutes, until the bread has heated through and is crisp. Serve at once.

garlic bread for one

serves 1

Mix together the garlic and oil and brush over the bread.
Put the bread under a hot grill (broiler) for 2–3 minutes,
until it is crisp on top and heated through.

$^1/_2$–1 garlic clove, peeled
and crushed (minced)
1tbsp olive oil
1 slice wholewheat bread

assorted crostini

These delicious, crisp slices of bread, and their colourful toppings, are very useful for parties or as snacks or appetizers. In keeping with the occasion, you can make them hearty – in true Tuscan style – or more delicate by varying the size and topping. A fairly slim french stick, sliced into rounds, slightly less than 1cm ($\frac{1}{2}$in) thick, makes a good, average-size crostini. For mini ones, you can use finger rolls, similarly sliced.

Preheat the oven to 150–160°C/275–300°F/Gas $\frac{3}{4}$–1. Put the rounds on baking sheets and bake for about 20–30 minutes, until they are dry and crisp. For a richer flavour, they may be brushed on both sides with olive oil, half-way through cooking, then returned to the oven. Let them cool on the baking sheets.

You can then serve the crostini as they are or add toppings such as any of the dips on pages 10–18, Tapenade (page 16), which is particularly good, or savoury vegetable pâté (available from healthfood shops), garnished with fresh herbs, pine nuts, capers, small pieces of grilled (broiled) sweet red pepper or olives as you wish. They are best assembled just before serving, so that the bread remains crisp, but all the toppings and garnishes can be prepared in advance so you are ready to put them together.

filled pitta bread

A pocket of pitta bread makes an excellent container. Fill it with your choice of ingredients, such as:

- shredded lettuce, sliced tomato, onion, avocado
- red kidney beans, cannellini beans or chickpeas (garbanzos)
- Coleslaw (page 33)
- Tabbouleh (page 126)
- Colourful Bean Salad (page 36)
- Felafel (page 98), mixed with shredded lettuce, tomato, cucumber, spring onion (scallion), grated carrot, moistened with vinaigrette and a topping of Tahini Dip (page 14)
- chilli aubergine (eggplant), slice half an aubergine (eggplant), brush with oil and grill (broil) for 6–7 minutes until tender, then mix with Tabasco or other chilli sauce
- chickpeas (garbanzos) or beansprouts mixed with torn lettuce leaves, sliced tomatoes, Hummus (page 13), coriander (cilantro) and black olives
- red beans with lettuce and Guacamole (page 15).

filled ciabatta

1 ciabatta, halved
lengthwise
2–4 lettuce leaves
1 beefsteak tomato, sliced
125g/4oz/^{3}/4 cup Hummus
(page 13) or Tahini Dip
(page 14), or vegan cheese,
sliced
1 small avocado, sliced
2 or 3 sprigs of fresh basil
salt
freshly ground black pepper

Arrange the filling ingredients in layers on one half of
the ciabatta, seasoning as you go. Put the other half
of ciabatta on top, then press down firmly and serve.

In order to make the best use of the space in this book, I decided not to include recipes for basic vegetable side dishes, which are naturally vegan. So there is no section on accompanying vegetables, only main vegetable dishes. When it came to salads, there were a few I had to include for various reasons – because they were particularly useful or nutritious, for example. I felt dressings also needed to be included, such as Vegan Mayonnaise (page 30), as well as a few appetizers, and being light, refreshing and based on fruit and vegetables, these complemented the salads and dressings (which can also be served as appetizers). Consequently these recipes work particularly well together.

salads, dressings and appetizers

vinaigrette

If you're making a bowlful of salad, it's easiest to put the ingredients for the dressing straight into the serving bowl but if you want to serve the dressing individually (in case not everyone likes it), it is handy to have some ready-made in a jar. You can vary the proportions of oil and vinegar according to taste but I prefer a simple, sharpish, not too oily vinaigrette, which is the basis of this recipe.

serves 6–8

1tsp sea salt
2–3 twists freshly ground
black pepper
2tbsp red wine vinegar
6tbsp olive oil

Put all the ingredients for the dressing into a clean, screw-top jar with a lid. Shake well until combined, then shake again before using.

mustard vinaigrette

This is a tangy dressing with a beautifully thick consistency – almost like mayonnaise. It's good when you want to add a real kick to a salad or it can be served with a main dish, such as Chestnut and Red Wine Pâté en Croûte (pages 74–5).

serves 4–6

Mix together the salt, mustard, vinegar and a good grinding of black pepper in a bowl.

Gradually whisk or stir in the oil, until blended, then add any other flavourings, if using.

1/2tsp sea salt
1tbsp good Dijon mustard
1tbsp red wine vinegar
freshly ground black pepper
3 tbsp good-quality olive oil,
preferably virgin
other flavouring
ingredients, such as garlic
and chopped herbs, if
desired, optional

vegan mayonnaise

This tastes very much like an egg-based mayonnaise and will keep for up to a week in a jar and stored in the fridge.

serves 4

4tbsp soya milk
1/4tsp mustard powder
salt
freshly ground black pepper
200ml/7fl oz/scant cup light olive oil, grapeseed or groundnut oil
1tbsp lemon juice
2–3tsp red wine vinegar

Mix together the soya milk, mustard powder and some seasoning. Gradually whisk in the oil. When the mixture starts to thicken, add the oil in a thin, steady stream, whisking continuously.

Add the lemon juice and vinegar and stir gently in one direction only. The mixture will become thicker as the acid has this effect on milk. Check the seasoning – this mayonnaise needs plenty of salt and pepper.

Tip: Should the mayonnaise curdle while you're making it, as with ordinary mayonnaise, you can easily remedy the situation. Put a tablespoonful of milk in a clean bowl and whisk in the curdled mixture, a little at a time. Funnily enough, I have just done exactly that while testing this recipe and it's fine!

variation

aioli

For this garlicky version of mayonnaise, crush (mince) 1–2 cloves garlic (or more if you like) and add it to the soya milk mixture as above.

mustard cream dressing

I love this dressing. It is thick and creamy, rather like mayonnaise or Greek yogurt, and is delicious served with hot dishes, such as crisp Lentil Chilli Burgers (page 103), as well as with salads.

serves 4

Put the mustard into a bowl, then gradually add the cream, stirring continuously. Add the vinegar and stir gently, in one direction, until the mixture has thickened.

Add the herbs, if using, season with a little salt and pepper, then cover and chill until needed.

2tsp Dijon mustard
250ml/8fl oz/1 cup soya cream
1tbsp red wine vinegar
1–2tbsp chopped fresh chives and/or parsley, optional
salt
freshly ground black pepper

gomasio

This Japanese seasoning is used instead of salt and is high in nutrients. It is excellent sprinkled over savoury dishes, as well as vegetables, grains, salads and as a dip for crudités.

makes 3–4
tablespoons

3–4tbsp sesame seeds
1tsp sea salt

Put the sesame seeds into a dry pan with the salt. Stir over a moderate heat for 1–2 minutes, until the seeds start to 'pop', smell roasted and brown a little. Leave to cool.

Grind the mixture to a powder in a coffee grinder or use a pestle and mortar.

variation

junior gomasio

For babies over one year old, use $6^{1}/_{2}$ tablespoons sesame seeds and 1 teaspoon of salt.

coleslaw

This vegan version is easy to make and is good served on its own as a salad as well as a topping or filling for baked potatoes, burgers and sandwiches.

Put all the ingredients into a bowl and mix together.

350g/12oz/3 cups white cabbage, finely shredded
100g/4oz/²/3 cup carrots, scraped and coarsely grated
4tbsp Vegan Mayonnaise or Vinaigrette or Mustard Vinaigrette, or Mustard Cream Dressing (pages 30, 28, 29 and 31)
salt
freshly ground black pepper

potato salad

700g/1$\frac{1}{2}$lb/4$\frac{1}{2}$ cups
potatoes, scrubbed or
peeled and cut into
even-sized pieces
4tbsp Vinaigrette, Vegan
Mayonnaise or Mustard
Cream Dressing (pages 28,
30 and 31),
salt
freshly ground black pepper
2–3tbsp chopped fresh
parsley or chives

Boil or steam the potatoes until they are just tender, then drain immediately. Allow the potatoes to cool slightly, cut them into smaller pieces if you wish, then put them into a bowl.

Add the dressing of your choice, salt, pepper and herbs. Stir gently until the potatoes are coated with the dressing.

tomato, black olive and red onion salad

I have included this light, colourful and refreshing salad because it seems to complement so many dishes. Indeed, I have suggested it as an accompaniment to several of the main course dishes in this book.

serves 4

Put the tomatoes, onions and olives into a bowl. Drizzle the olive oil over them and season with salt and pepper. Add the basil, if using. Leave to stand for 30 minutes or longer, stirring occasionally, to give the flavours a chance to blend.

700g/1^1/2lb/4 cups firm tomatoes, sliced
1 red onion, sliced
125g/4oz/1 cup pitted black olives
1–2tbsp olive oil
salt
freshly ground black pepper
1–2 leafy sprigs of fresh basil, leaves torn or roughly chopped, optional

colourful bean salad

This attractive bean salad makes a useful appetizer or side dish, or a great main course served with some warm rolls or bread and perhaps a green salad.

serves 6

1tbsp Dijon mustard
1tbsp red wine vinegar
3tbsp olive oil
salt
freshly ground black pepper
425g/15oz can cannellini or butter beans (lima beans), drained, or 100g/3^{1}/$_{2}$oz/^{1}/$_{2}$ cup dried beans
425g/15oz can red kidney beans, drained or 100 g/3^{1}/$_{2}$oz/^{1}/$_{2}$ cup dried beans
125g/4oz/generous ^{1}/$_{2}$ cup sweetcorn (fresh, raw kernels cut from a cob or frozen sweetcorn, thawed)
12 black olives, halved and pitted
1 small sweet red pepper, deseeded and finely chopped
2 heaped tbsp chopped fresh parsley

If using dried beans, soak and cook them as described on page 97, then drain.

Put the mustard, vinegar and oil into a large bowl with some salt and pepper and whisk together until combined. Add the beans to the bowl with all the remaining ingredients and mix gently until amalgamated.

cucumber, radish and hiziki salad

Seaweeds – or sea vegetables as they are often called – are a rich source of nutrients. The leading vegan doctor and American general practitioner, Dr Michael Klaper, recommends in his table of nutrients (page xiii) that we include seaweed in our diet 2–3 times a week. This recipe, which uses hiziki, is a very pleasant way to do so. Hiziki is a delicate seaweed, which you can buy at some health food shops and stockists of Japanese foods. These places should also stock rice vinegar, although you could use a dash of wine or cider vinegar diluted with a little water instead.

serves 4

Wash the hiziki, then put it into a saucepan, cover with water, and simmer for 5–15 minutes, until it has softened enough for your taste. Drain.

Put the cucumber and radishes into a bowl and add the vinegar, sugar, and salt and pepper to taste. Mix well.

small handful of hiziki
1 cucumber, peeled and diced
1 bunch radishes, trimmed and sliced
1–2tbsp rice vinegar or
$^1/_2$–1tbsp wine or cider vinegar, diluted with the same amount of water
sugar
salt
freshly ground black pepper

pears with mustard cream dressing

Really good, ripe pears make all the difference to this delicious appetizer. I generally buy them when they're hard, up to a week in advance, and allow them to ripen at room temperature so that they are at that stage of ripeness when you can slice them quite easily with a fork.

serves 6

2tsp Dijon mustard
250ml/8fl oz/1 cup soya cream
1tbsp tarragon vinegar
salt
freshly ground black pepper
3 large, ripe dessert pears, preferably Comice
2tbsp lemon juice
12 lettuce leaves
mild paprika
6 sprigs of tarragon, to garnish, optional

First, make the tarragon cream. Put the mustard into a bowl, then gradually add the cream, stirring continuously. Add the vinegar and stir gently, in one direction, until the mixture has thickened. Season with a little salt and pepper, then cover and chill until needed.

Just before you want to serve the dish, halve and peel the pears, and carefully remove the cores (a teaspoon is good for doing this). Brush the pears with lemon juice. Put two lettuce leaves on each plate and place a pear, core-side down, on top.

Spoon some of the tarragon cream over each of the pears, then sprinkle with a little paprika and garnish with a sprig of tarragon, if using. Serve at once.

avocado, orange and grapefruit

A pretty and refreshing combination.

serves 4–6

Carefully scoop out the avocado flesh using a spoon. Slice the flesh, then put it into a bowl and mix with the lemon juice.

Hold the grapefruit over the bowl and cut off the peel and pith using a sharp knife. Then cut the segments of flesh away from the transparent skin. When all the segments have been removed, squeeze the bits of grapefruit still attached to the skin over the bowl to extract all the juice before discarding.

Peel and segment the oranges in the same way as the grapefruit and add them to the bowl. Taste the mixture and sweeten with a little sugar, if necessary.

Serve on individual plates or in bowls and garnish with the watercress.

3 avocados, halved and stoned
2tbsp lemon juice
1 large grapefruit
2 large oranges
sugar, to taste, if necessary
$1/2$ bunch of watercress, to garnish

sweet red and yellow pepper salad

Grilled (broiled) sweet pepper halves make a very good appetizer. The filling provides plenty of possibilities for variety: here I've filled them with tomatoes, courgettes (zucchini) and basil, but you could try fried mushrooms, cubes of ripe avocado, artichoke hearts or feta cheese with red onion rings.

serves 4

2 sweet red peppers

2 sweet yellow peppers

450g/1lb/4 cups courgettes (zucchini), thinly sliced

2tbsp olive oil

450g/1lb/2$\frac{1}{2}$ cups cherry tomatoes, halved

2 cloves garlic, crushed (minced)

salt

freshly ground black pepper

4 sprigs of basil, to garnish

Heat the grill (broiler). Meanwhile, halve the peppers, cutting right through the stem. Remove the core and seeds, being careful not to loosen the stem.

Place the pepper halves, shiny-side up, under the grill (broiler) and cook for 10–15 minutes, until they are tender and charred in places. Remove and set aside.

Lay the courgette (zucchini) slices on a large plate, drizzle the olive oil over them and turn them with your fingers so that they are coated in the oil. Grill (broil) the courgettes (zucchini) for 5–10 minutes, until they have browned and are tender. Transfer the courgette (zucchini) slices to a bowl.

Put the tomatoes under the grill (broiler) for about 5 minutes, or until they are tender and charred in places. You can take off their skins or leave them, as you prefer, then add them to the courgettes (zucchini).

Add the garlic to the courgettes (zucchini) and tomatoes and season with salt and pepper to taste. Mix gently, then spoon the mixture into the pepper halves. Serve warm or at room temperature – one yellow pepper half and one red one on each plate, garnished with a sprig of fresh basil.

mushroom pâté with porcini

The dried porcini mushrooms, which are quite widely available, give this pâté an intense mushroomy flavour. Yet, if you can't get them, you can still make and enjoy this pâté. A food processor is helpful when making this recipe since there is a lot of chopping involved.

serves 4–6

First, put the porcini into a cup, cover with 2–3 tablespoons of boiling water, then leave to soak for 10–15 minutes. Drain, reserving the liquid, and chop the porcini.

Heat the margarine in a large saucepan and add the onion and garlic. Cover the pan and cook gently for 5 minutes, until the onion begins to soften. Add the mushrooms to the pan, along with the chopped porcini and their liquid, and cook, uncovered, for 10–15 minutes, until the mushrooms are tender and all the liquid has evaporated.

Add the Madeira and cook for a further 1–2 minutes, then remove from the heat.

Coarsely chop the mixture in a food processor – don't let it become too smooth. Season with salt and freshly ground black pepper to taste. Put the mixture into a serving bowl or a 450g (1lb) loaf tin (pan) or individual ramekins and leave to cool, then store it in the fridge until you are ready to serve.

Serve the pâté cold but not straight from the fridge. If you have used a loaf tin or ramekins, run a knife around the edge of the pâté and turn out on a serving plate or side plates, as desired.

10g/¼oz dried porcini or cep mushrooms
50g/2oz/4tbsp vegan margarine
1 small onion, finely chopped
1 clove garlic, crushed (minced)
700g/1½lb/8 cups mushrooms, wiped and thickly sliced
1–2tbsp Madeira, sherry or brandy
salt
freshly ground black pepper

sauces

A good sauce can make all the difference to a meal, adding the perfect finishing touch. Here is a selection of some of the best, including vegan versions of basics such as gravy and white sauce, some new classics, including a confit and a salsa, and my favourites for special occasions, including vegan versions of hollandaise and béarnaise sauce.

bread sauce

Here is a vegan version of this traditional favourite and Christmas classic. It goes well with one of the festive savoury pastries on pages 56–79, Lentil Bake (page 111), which I love despite – or perhaps because of – its simplicity, and the traditional Nut Roast (pages 130–1).

serves 6

Stick the cloves into the onion and put into a saucepan with the bay leaf and soya milk. Bring to the boil, then remove from the heat, cover, and leave for 1–2 hours for the flavours to infuse.

Add the breadcrumbs and margarine, then mix well. Cook over a very low heat for 15 minutes, then cover and leave until just before you are ready to serve.

Just before serving, remove the onion and bay leaf, stir in the cream and some salt, pepper and freshly grated nutmeg to taste.

8 cloves
1 onion
1 bay leaf
300ml/10fl oz/1^{1}/$_{4}$ cups soya milk
50g/2oz/1 cup fresh white breadcrumbs
15g/^{1}/$_{2}$oz/1tbsp vegan margarine
2–4tbsp vegan cream
salt
freshly ground black pepper
freshly grated nutmeg, to taste

cranberry sauce

Another festive sauce that goes well with the dishes suggested in the recipe for Bread Sauce (page 43). These served with crisp, golden roast potatoes, some nice old-fashioned Vegan Gravy (page 45) and Brussels sprouts and you have a perfect Christmas dinner. This recipe makes a lot of sauce, but it keeps well in the fridge – for several weeks, if you wish.

serves 6–8

175g/6oz/1^{1}/2 cups fresh cranberries

4tbsp water

75g/3oz/generous cup sugar

juice and grated zest of 1 well-scrubbed orange

Rinse the cranberries and remove any damaged ones. Put them into a saucepan with the water, cover, and cook gently for 4–5 minutes, until the cranberries are tender. Add the sugar and cook over a low heat until the granules have dissolved.

Remove from the heat and add the orange juice and zest and leave to cool – the mixture will thicken as it cools. Reheat gently before serving.

vegan gravy

A really tasty thin gravy which freezes well. If, however, you prefer a thick gravy, simply adjust the amount of liquid you use until it is just how you like it. I like to freeze the gravy in convenient small portions, so I always have some to hand for gravy-lovers.

Heat the oil in a medium-sized saucepan, then add the flour and stir for a few minutes until the flour becomes nut brown in colour. Remove from the heat and stir in the gravy powder and garlic.

Return to the heat and gradually add the water, stirring all the time, until thick and smooth. Add the soy sauce and salt and pepper to taste.

2tbsp oil

25g/1oz/2tbsp wholewheat flour

4tsp gravy powder (not granules, and read the ingredients to check it is meat-free)

2 cloves garlic, crushed (minced)

600ml/1 pint/2^{1}/2 cups water

1tbsp soy sauce

salt

freshly ground black pepper

wild mushroom sauce

A smart sauce with a touch of grandeur. Serve it with something like Lentil Bake (page 111) for an instant upgrade to luxury class.

serves 4–6

10g/¼oz dried porcini or cep mushrooms
600ml/1 pint/2½ cups water
1 small onion, thinly sliced
1tbsp olive oil
2tsp cornflour (cornstarch)
2tbsp Madeira
1tbsp soy sauce or tamari
salt
freshly ground black pepper

Wash the porcini to remove any grit, then put them in the water. Bring to the boil and leave to soak for 30–60 minutes, until softened. Drain, reserving the liquid, then chop the porcini.

Meanwhile, fry the onion in the oil for 10 minutes, until browned. Add the porcini and simmer for 30 minutes, until tender.

Mix the cornflour (cornstarch) with the Madeira and soy sauce and add to the mushroom mixture. Bring to the boil to thicken slightly. Season with salt and pepper to taste.

fresh tomato sauce

Simple, bright, fresh-tasting and low in fat, this sauce never disappoints, and is as good over pasta as it is with pastry, bean, vegetable or nut dishes.

serves 4

Heat the oil in a medium-sized saucepan. Add the onion and sauté, covered, for 5 minutes. Add the tomatoes, basil and garlic, stir, then cover and simmer for 15–20 minutes.

If using canned tomatoes, the sauce can be served as is or blended in a blender or food processor. If using fresh tomatoes, liquidize the sauce, then strain it into a clean pan to remove the tomato skins. Season with salt and pepper to taste.

1tbsp olive oil
1 onion, chopped
450g/1lb/2^{1}/2 cups fresh tomatoes or 425g/15oz canned tomatoes, chopped
2 sprigs of fresh basil, chopped
1 large clove garlic, crushed (minced)
salt
freshly ground black pepper

white sauce

Soya milk can be used instead of cow's milk to make a creamy and delicious white sauce. The quantity of soya milk used depends on how thick you desire the sauce – just add enough milk to make it the consistency you want.

serves 4

2tbsp soya oil
25g/1oz/2tbsp plain (all-purpose) flour
300ml/10fl oz/1$\frac{1}{4}$ cups soya milk
salt
freshly ground black pepper
freshly grated nutmeg

Heat the oil in a saucepan and add the flour. Stir over a gentle heat for a moment or two, but don't let the flour brown. Add a third of the milk, stir until thickened, then add another third, stir until thickened, then add the rest of the milk and stir until smooth. The sauce will become thicker as it cooks, and you can always add more soya milk after cooking if necessary.

Heat the sauce over a very gentle heat for 10 minutes, to cook the flour. Add more soya milk, if necessary, and season with salt, pepper and nutmeg, to taste.

variations

parsley sauce

Stir 1–2 tablespoons chopped fresh parsley into the sauce just before serving.

béchamel sauce

For this delicately flavoured white sauce, first flavour the milk by heating it in a pan
with a small piece of peeled raw onion, a piece of carrot, a celery stick, if you have one,
a bay leaf and a few parsley stalks and sprigs of thyme, if available. Bring to the boil,
then remove from the heat, cover, and leave for at least 15 minutes, for the flavours to
infuse. Then strain, discard the vegetables and herbs and use the milk to make a sauce
as described above.

low-fat white sauce

This sauce is both low in fat and calories. You can use cornflour (cornstarch), or arrowroot or potato flour, which are preferred by health experts.

serves 4

1tbsp arrowroot, potato flour or cornflour (cornstarch)
300ml/10fl oz/1¼ cups soya milk
1 bay leaf, optional
salt
freshly ground pepper
freshly grated nutmeg

Put the arrowroot, potato flour or cornflour (cornstarch) into a bowl and mix to a thin paste with some of the soya milk.

Put the rest of the soya milk into a saucepan with the bay leaf, if using, and bring to the boil. Pour the boiling milk over the mixture in the bowl, stir, then return it to the saucepan and stir over a gentle heat for 1–2 minutes, until the sauce has thickened. Season with salt, pepper and nutmeg. Remove the bay leaf just before serving (it can be washed, dried and used again if you wish).

variations

This sauce can be flavoured in many different ways, including chopped parsley, as suggested for the White Sauce (page 48); chopped fresh herbs such as chives, tarragon, dill or fennel; chopped spring onions (scallions), fennel or celery stems and leaves; finely chopped or sliced very fresh raw mushrooms; or chopped and cooked asparagus. Add these flavourings in the final stages of cooking.

horseradish sauce

Most of the ready-made horseradish sauces and relishes contain dairy products, but grated horseradish is a suitable alternative.

Gently mix the Mustard Cream Dressing with enough grated horseradish to give the sauce a good tang – start with $1/2$ a teaspoonful, adding more if you wish. Season to taste with salt.

1 quantity Mustard Cream Dressing (page 31)
grated horseradish, to taste
salt

tomato salsa

A salsa is a kind of raw relish, which can be made from any finely chopped fresh fruits and vegetables, lubricated with vinegar, juice or oil, and flavoured with ingredients such as herbs, spices or capers. You can continue to add ingredients until you have a combination that tastes right to you, aiming for a balance between the different flavours, colours and textures. A salsa can add a fresh and colourful note to almost any dish. Here is a basic recipe for you to try.

serves 4

4 tomatoes, chopped
1 onion, preferably red, chopped
2tbsp red wine vinegar
4tbsp chopped fresh coriander (cilantro)
1 green chilli, deseeded and finely sliced
salt
freshly ground black pepper

Put the tomatoes and onion into a bowl with the vinegar, coriander (cilantro), chilli and salt and pepper to taste. Stir and leave to stand for 10 minutes, or longer, for the flavours to develop. Check the seasoning and serve.

variations

A little crushed (minced) garlic can be added or chopped avocado, fresh mango or cucumber. You can use lime or lemon juice instead of some or all of the vinegar, and a little of the grated zest. Try using different herbs such as fresh mint, flat-leaf parsley, lovage or thyme, or add some capers or finely chopped sun-dried tomatoes. The possibilities are endless.

lemon and parsley sauce

A tangy, bright green sauce, which is served cold and is good with vegan burgers.

Combine the parsley, garlic, lemon juice and oil, whisking well to make a dressing. It will thicken a little as the oil and lemon juice emulsify. Season with salt and pepper.

40g/1^1/$_2$oz/^{3}/$_4$ cup fresh
parsley, tough stems
removed and finely chopped
1 clove garlic, peeled
juice of 1 lemon
6tbsp olive oil
salt
freshly ground black pepper

confit of red onions

This dish goes very well with bean and lentil bakes and burgers (pages 98, 99, 103, 104, 108, 111). The confit can be made in advance and gently warmed through before serving.

serves 4

2tbsp olive oil

450g/1lb/4 cups red onions, chopped

300ml/10fl oz/1¼ cups red wine

50g/2oz/generous ⅓ cup demerara (coarse light brown) or granulated (superfine) sugar

4tbsp red wine vinegar

salt

freshly ground black pepper

Heat the oil in a medium-sized saucepan. Add the onions, cover, and cook gently for 10 minutes, stirring occasionally.

Add the wine, sugar and vinegar. Bring to the boil, then reduce the heat and leave it to simmer very gently, uncovered, for 45–60 minutes, until the onion is very tender and the mixture syrupy. Season with salt and plenty of black pepper. Serve warm.

quick vegan hollandaise sauce

This rich and creamy sauce is very similar to the traditional egg-based Hollandaise sauce. Make it just before serving or keep it warm in a vacuum flask or put it in a bowl placed in a roasting tin of gently steaming water.

serves 4–6

125g/4oz/1/2 cup vegan margarine
2tbsp soya milk
juice of 1 lemon
salt
freshly ground black pepper

Put the margarine into a small saucepan and heat gently until it has melted, but do not allow it to brown.

Meanwhile, put the soya milk and lemon juice into a food processor or blender and season with salt and pepper. With the food processor or blender on, pour the melted margarine in a steady stream in through the top of the goblet. The mixture will start to thicken when you have added about two-thirds or three-quarters of the margarine. Continue adding the remaining margarine, then return the mixture to the pan, taste and serve or keep warm until needed.

variation

vegan béarnaise sauce

For this tangy variation, which is good with vegan burgers, put 1 tablespoonful of finely chopped onion or shallot into a small saucepan with 1 1/2 tablespoons of red wine vinegar and the same quantity of water. Bring to the boil and cook until almost all the liquid has evaporated. Cool, then stir it into the Hollandaise.

pastry dishes

Pastry dishes make substantial, attractive and popular main courses. For everyday pastry dishes, I like to make an easy shortcrust (piecrust) using wholewheat flour, because of the extra nutrients it contains. Puff pastry (flaky piecrust) – a bought one made with pure vegetable fat – makes a nice change and is excellent for special occasions such as Christmas. Filo is another option, brushed with olive oil between the layers to make a delicious, dill-flavoured vegan version of Spanakopita.

There are also endless possibilities for quiche fillings and replacements for egg-custard mixtures. You can avoid the custard altogether, as in the classic Pissaladière Niçoise (page 69), or create variations based on grilled (broiled) or roasted vegetables. You could make a base using puréed vegetables, including bright herbs and whole vegetables in the purée, or you could try a dip – such as Tahini Dip, Hummus or Sweet Red Pepper and Garlic Dip (pages 14, 13 and 17) – as a base and decorate it with baby vegetables, herbs, olives or even edible flowers.

Here, too, you will find the tried and tested and much-loved recipe for Spiced Potato and Chickpea (Garbanzo) Pasties (Turnovers), and delicious home-made Pizza, which is well worth the effort as it trounces ready-made versions.

flaky potato pie

This pie, with its creamy layers of potato encased in crisp flaky pastry, is excellent hot but is also surprisingly good cold, making it a perfect choice for a picnic.

serves 4–6

Put the cream into a large saucepan with the thyme and heat gently. When it comes to the boil, cover, and remove from the heat.

Meanwhile, rinse the potatoes in cold water and drain, then add to the cream, along with the garlic. Bring to the boil, then simmer gently for 4–5 minutes. Remove from the heat and season with salt, pepper and nutmeg, then leave to cool.

Preheat the oven to 230°C/450°F/Gas 8 and put a baking sheet in the centre. Roll out two-thirds of the pastry and line a 20cm (8in) diameter x 2.5cm (2in) deep, flan tin (tart pan) with a removable base.

Check the seasoning of the potato mixture, then arrange it in the pastry case and brush the edges with cold water.

Roll out the rest of the pastry until it is large enough to cover the top, then lay it over the flan tin (tart pan) and trim and crimp (ruffle) the edges. Make a steam-hole in the centre. Brush with a little soya milk, then bake for 10 minutes. Reduce the oven to 170°C/325°F/Gas 3 and bake for a further 40–45 minutes, until the pie is golden and risen and the potato feels tender when tested with the blade of a sharp knife.

2 × 250ml/8fl oz packets of soya cream
2–3 sprigs of thyme
500g/1lb 2oz/$3^1/2$ cups potatoes, peeled and thinly sliced
1 clove garlic, crushed (minced)
salt
freshly ground black pepper
freshly grated nutmeg
350g/12oz bought frozen puff pastry (flaky pastry), defrosted
a little soya milk, for glazing

spring rolls with dipping sauce

These can be prepared in advance as they freeze well and heated from frozen. Serve the spring rolls with some cooked rice and a spring onion (scallion) salad for a complete meal or take them out of the freezer as you need them and fry, grill (broil) or bake for a quick snack.

makes 12

1tbsp olive oil
1 onion, chopped
175g/6oz/heaped cup carrot, coarsely grated
1 sweet green pepper, deseeded and sliced
2 cloves garlic, crushed (minced)
1 green chilli, deseeded and finely sliced
175g/6oz/3 cups beansprouts
1tbsp tamari
salt
freshly ground black pepper
12 sheets filo pastry
oil, for deep-frying

Heat the oil in a large frying pan. Add the onion, carrot and green pepper and fry for 7 minutes, until almost soft. Add the garlic, chilli and beansprouts and fry for a further 2–3 minutes, until all the vegetables are cooked.

Add the tamari and season with salt and pepper, then leave to cool.

Fold a sheet of filo pastry in half. Place a good heap of the vegetable mixture just inside one corner, fold over the corner, then the edges, and roll up, to make a neat parcel. Repeat with the remaining sheets of filo.

Half-fill a saucepan or deep frying pan with oil. Heat until the oil forms bubbles around the tip of a wooden chopstick or handle of a wooden spoon when inserted in the oil.

Meanwhile, make the dipping sauce by mixing together all the ingredients. Put it into a small bowl.

Deep-fry the spring rolls, a few at a time, for about 4 minutes, until golden brown and crisp. Drain on kitchen

paper. Keep warm while you fry the remaining spring
rolls. Serve with the dipping sauce.

   Alternatively, preheat the oven to 200°C/400°F/Gas 6.
Place the spring rolls on a lightly oiled baking sheet.
Brush the spring rolls lightly with olive oil and bake for
about 30 minutes, turning them after about 20 minutes,
until both sides are cooked and crisp. Leave to cool, then
freeze. To heat the spring rolls from frozen, bake them for
25–30 minutes at 200°C/ 400°F/Gas 6 or in a microwave
for 5–7 minutes (refer to the manufacturer's manual).

for the dipping sauce:
1/2 small onion, finely
chopped
2tbsp soy sauce
2tsp rice vinegar or 1tsp
wine vinegar and 1tsp
water
2tsp caster sugar
(granulated sugar)
2tsp sesame oil

samosas

Serve these samosas with mango chutney and a tomato and onion salad or, for a more substantial meal, with steamed brown rice or spiced rice. You can brush the samosas with oil and bake them, although deep-frying produces the best results, though obviously is more calorific. However, this is offset by the fact that the dough does not contain as much fat as normal pastry.

makes 32

225g/8oz/2 cups plain (all-purpose) wholewheat flour
$^1/_2$tsp salt
$^1/_2$tsp baking powder
4tbsp soya oil
about 7tbsp water

for the filling:
1 large onion, chopped
2tbsp soya oil, plus extra for deep-frying
1 large clove garlic, crushed (minced)
1tsp grated fresh root ginger
1tsp ground cumin
1tsp ground coriander
700g/1$^1/_2$lb/4$^1/_2$ cups potatoes, cooked and diced
225g/8oz/1$^1/_2$ cups frozen peas, thawed
salt
freshly ground black pepper

First, make the pastry: put the flour, salt and baking powder into a bowl, then add the oil and just enough of the water to make a soft, but not sticky dough. Knead the dough for 5 minutes, then wrap in foil and chill for 30 minutes.

Meanwhile, make the filling, fry the onion in the oil for 8 minutes, until soft but not browned. Add the garlic, ginger, cumin and coriander and cook for a further 2 minutes. Mix in the potatoes and peas, season, then remove from the heat and leave to cool.

Remove the dough from the fridge and divide into 16 pieces. On a lightly floured board, roll each piece into a circle, about 15cm/6in diameter. Pile the circles on top of one another, then cut them in half to make 32 half circles.

Take one of the half circles of pastry and brush the cut edges with water, then fold it in half and press the moistened cut edges firmly together to form a cone. Fill the cone with a heaped teaspoon of the filling, then moisten the top and fold over to enclose the filling. Make the rest of the samosas in the same way.

Heat sufficient oil in a pan or deep frying pan to 180°C/350°F, or when bubbles immediately form around a wooden spoon handle or a chopstick dipped into the oil. Add enough samosas to make a single layer, letting them cook slowly and turning them so that they become brown and crisp. Drain them on absorbent kitchen paper. Serve them hot, warm or at room temperature.

basic shortcrust pastry (piecrust)

Shortcrust pastry (piecrust) is not nearly as difficult to make as many people imagine. In fact, it's quite quick and easy – especially if you have a food processor – and worth while as a pastry case can make the basis of many excellent dishes. You can also freeze the pastry at one of three stages: as a dough before rolling out; as a "raw" case before baking; or cooked and ready for filling. This is a good basic pastry, which is very light and delicious. The olive oil adds richness to the pastry and also seems to make it more malleable.

makes 2 shallow 20–23cm/8–9in pastry cases

200g/7oz/1²/₃ cups plain (all-purpose) wholewheat flour
pinch of salt
100g/3¹/₂oz/scant ¹/₂ cup vegan margarine
2–3tbsp olive oil

Sift the flour into a large bowl or the bowl of your food processor, adding the bran left in the sieve (sifter). Add the salt and margarine. Rub (cut), or process, the margarine into the flour until the mixture forms breadcrumbs.

Mix the oil with 3 tablespoons of cold water and add to the bowl. Mix or process briefly until a dough forms. Wrap the dough in clingfilm (plastic wrap) or foil and chill for at least 30 minutes before using.

To make 2 pastry cases, preheat the oven to 200°C/400°F/Gas 6 and grease 2 x 20–22cm/8–9in flan tins (tart pans).

Divide the dough into 2 equal-sized pieces and roll each one into a flat ball. Roll each ball out thinly to fit the flan tins (tart pans). Press the pastry down into the tins (pans) and trim the edges. Prick the bases all over with a fork. If the sides of the flan tins (tart pans) are high, place a piece of greased foil in each tin (pan), positioning it so that it presses against the sides. Weigh down the foil with dried beans to hold the sides up.

Bake for 8–10 minutes, until the pastry has firmed. Remove the foil and beans and cook for a further 8–10 minutes, until the pastry has browned lightly and is shrinking away from the sides of the tin (pan). Remove the pastry cases from their tins (pans) and place them on a wire rack to cool. This helps them to stay crisp.

onion and fresh herb quiche

The custard in this flan (quiche) is made from tofu, flavoured with onion and garlic and whizzed to a creamy consistency. Here this basic topping is poured over onions and fresh herbs, but many other ingredients can also be used – see just some of the possibilities given under Variations at the end of the recipe.

serves 4

1 × 20–23cm/8–9in baked
pastry case (page 62)

for the filling:
1tbsp olive oil
2 onions, chopped
1 clove garlic, crushed
(minced)
1 packet tofu
2tbsp (heaped) chopped
fresh herbs
1tbsp good-quality soy
sauce or tamari
salt
freshly ground black pepper
freshly grated nutmeg

Preheat the oven to 180°C/350°F/Gas 4 and place a baking sheet in the centre of the oven.

To make the filling, heat the oil in a frying pan. Add the onions and gently fry for 10 minutes. Put half the onions into a liquidizer and blend with the garlic and tofu. Add the fresh herbs, soy sauce and salt and pepper to taste. Mix in the rest of the fried onions.

Spoon the mixture in the pastry case, spreading it out evenly. Place the quiche on the baking sheet and bake for 20–25 minutes, until heated through and set.

variations

mushroom flan (quiche)

Replace one of the onions with 100g/4oz/1^1/$_2$ cups button mushrooms, thinly sliced. Liquidize the tofu with *all* the fried onions, rather than just half of them. Fry the mushrooms separately, then add them to the liquidized tofu mixture and use this to fill the pastry case.

sweetcorn quiche

Use just 1 fried onion and liquidize it with the tofu. Add 100g/4oz/generous $^1/_2$ cup frozen sweetcorn kernels and use to fill the pastry case.

quick mint and pea quiche

Use just 1 fried onion and liquidize it with the tofu. Add 100g/4oz/1 cup frozen peas and 2 tablespoons of finely chopped mint and then use to fill the pastry case.

asparagus quiche

Use just 1 fried onion and liquidize it with the tofu. Add 225g/8oz/8 spears cooked fresh asparagus, cut into even-sized lengths, and then use to fill the pastry case.

ratatouille quiche

Make the quiche as described above, but use good, thick, tasty ratatouille in place of the onions.

broccoli and almond quiche

The filling in this quiche consists of lightly cooked broccoli in a creamy béchamel sauce with a topping of crisp, flaked (slivered) almonds. Other combinations of cooked vegetables and nuts can be used and some suggestions can be found at the end of this recipe.

serves 4–6 as a main course, 6–8 as an appetizer

1 × 20–23cm/8–9in baked pastry case (page 62)

for the filling:
700g/1^{1}/2lb broccoli, trimmed and cut into even-sized florets
1 quantity Béchamel Sauce (page 49)
salt
freshly ground black pepper
freshly grated nutmeg
25g/1oz/^{1}/3 cup flaked (slivered) almonds

Preheat the oven to 200°C/400°F/Gas 6 and place a baking sheet in the centre. Lightly grease a 20cm/8in flan tin (tart pan).

Cook the broccoli in 2.5cm (1in) of boiling water for 4–5 minutes, until just tender. Drain and mix with the Béchamel Sauce. Season with salt, pepper and grated nutmeg.

Spoon the mixture into the pastry case, sprinkle the almonds over the top and bake for 15–20 minutes, until set and the almonds are golden.

variations

avocado and pine nut quiche

Replace the broccoli and almonds with 2 avocados, skinned and cut into chunks, and pine nuts. Sprinkle the avocado with the juice of a lemon then fold it into the sauce. Season with a crushed (minced) clove garlic, a good pinch of chilli powder or curry powder or a few drops of Tabasco. Sprinkle the pine nuts over the top and bake as above.

mushroom and pine nut quiche

Replace the broccoli and almonds with 350g/12oz/4 cups sliced button mushrooms, oyster mushrooms or wild mushrooms, lightly fried in 1 tablespoon of olive oil.

spiced potato turnovers

makes 4

1 quantity Basic Shortcrust
Pastry (Piecrust), (page 62)
a little soya milk, to glaze

for the filling:
2tbsp olive oil
1 onion, chopped
225g/8oz/1^{1}/2 cups
potatoes, peeled and
cut into 5mm/^{1}/4in dice
1tbsp ground coriander
1tsp ground cumin
425g/15oz can chickpeas
(garbanzos), drained
salt
freshly ground black pepper

To make the filling, fry the onion in the oil for 5 minutes, then add the potatoes, coriander and cumin. Stir, then cook gently, covered, stirring from time to time, for 10–15 minutes, until the potatoes are tender.

Remove from the heat and add the chickpeas (garbanzos). Season to taste with salt and pepper. Leave to cool.

Preheat the oven to 200°C/400°F/Gas 6 and lightly grease a large baking sheet.

Divide the pastry into 4 equal-sized pieces, then roll each one into a circle on a lightly floured board, about 15cm (6in) across. Spoon a quarter of the potato mixture into the centre of a circle, then fold up the sides of the pastry and press the edges together over the filling to make a turnover shape.

Put the pastie onto the prepared baking sheet and brush with soya milk, then make a couple of holes each side of the join at the top to let the steam out. Repeat to make 3 more turnovers. Bake for 20–25 minutes, until brown and crisp.

pissaladière niçoise

This version of the classic French dish avoids anchovies in favour of strips of sweet peppers. However, the filling retains the onions, which are fried in olive oil until meltingly tender. You could also add other vegetables, such as slices of aubergine (eggplant) or courgette (zucchini) or mushrooms.

serves 4

Heat the oil in a frying pan. Add the onions and thyme and cook gently, covered, stirring from time to time, for 30 minutes. Add the garlic and cook for a further 10 minutes, until the onion is very soft and sweet. Season with salt and pepper to taste.

Meanwhile preheat the grill (broil) to high. Grill (broil) the peppers for 10–15 minutes, until they are tender and the skin has blackened and blistered in places. Remove from the grill (broiler), cover with a plate and leave until cool enough to handle, then peel off the skin. Cut the flesh into strips.

Preheat the oven to 180°C/350°F/Gas 4, placing a baking sheet in the centre.

Spoon the onion mixture into the pastry case, smoothing the top, then arrange the strips of pepper and olives on top. Bake for 15–20 minutes, until heated through. This dish is good hot, warm or cold.

1 × 20–23cm/8–9in baked pastry case (page 62)

for the filling:
4tbsp olive oil
4 large onions, preferably red, thinly sliced
2–3 sprigs of thyme
2 cloves garlic, crushed (minced)
1 sweet red pepper, deseeded and quartered
1 sweet yellow pepper, deseeded and quartered
salt
freshly ground black pepper
a few black olives

spanikopita

This vegan version of the Greek classic is very good served with a tomato, onion, cucumber and black olive salad. I find a shallow round tin – like a flan tin (tart pan) – is best for this because it gives the neatest slices.

serves 4–6

olive oil, for brushing

10 sheets filo pastry

500g/1lb 2oz/9 cups frozen spinach or fresh spinach, trimmed, cooked, drained and cooled

bunch of spring onions (scallions), trimmed and chopped

2tbsp chopped fresh dill

salt

freshly ground black pepper

Preheat the oven to 200°C/400°F/Gas 6. Brush a deep pie dish (tart pan) generously with olive oil, then place a sheet of filo pastry in it, allowing the edges to hang over the sides of the dish. Brush with olive oil, then place another sheet of filo pastry on top at right angles to the first sheet. Continue in this way, using 5 sheets of filo pastry. (Keep the rest covered with a damp cloth to prevent them drying out.)

Mix together the spinach, spring onions (scallions) and dill and season to taste with salt and pepper. Spoon this mixture on top of the filo.

Cover with the rest of the filo, laying the sheets in different directions and brushing each sheet with olive oil as before, and finish by brushing with olive oil. Neaten the sides, then prick and decorate the top with crumpled pieces of pastry, brushed with oil. Bake for 30–40 minutes, until golden.

flaky mushroom roll

This favourite recipe is based on the Russian dish, coulibiac. It's good served with a sauce made by adding chopped fresh dill to the Mustard Cream Dressing (page 31) as well as a variety of vegetables.

serves 6

Preheat the oven to 230°C/450°F/Gas 8. Melt the margarine in a large saucepan and fry the onion for 10 minutes. Add the mushrooms and fry for 15–20 minutes, until the liquid has evaporated. Remove from the heat, add the parsley, garlic, rice and plenty of seasoning. Leave to cool.

Roll out the pastry and make 2 strips, the first measuring about 15 x 30 cm (6 x 12in), the second 20–23 x 30 cm (8–9 x 12in). Place the first strip on a baking sheet which has been brushed with cold water. Spoon the mushroom mixture over the pastry, leaving a 1cm ($^{1}/_{2}$in) gap around the edge. Pile up the mushroom mixture to form a loaf-like shape. Brush the edges of the pastry with cold water, then lay the second piece of pastry over the top of the mixture, aligning the edges, then press down lightly to seal. Trim the edges. Cut the trimmings into decorative shapes, if you wish, and stick them on top of the pastry with water. Make a few small steam holes with a fork or skewer, then brush with soya milk, to glaze, if you wish.

Bake for 10 minutes, then reduce the oven to 200°C/400°F/Gas 6 and bake for a further 20–25 minutes, until the pastry is golden, crisp and flaky. Serve at once.

25g/1oz/2tbsp vegan margarine
1 onion, chopped
225g/8oz/3 cups mushrooms, washed and chopped
2tbsp chopped fresh parsley
2 cloves garlic, crushed (minced)
100g/4oz/generous $^{1}/_{2}$ cup (raw weight) brown rice, cooked
sea salt
freshly ground black pepper
350g/12oz frozen puff pastry (flaky pastry), defrosted
soya milk, for glazing

Ann's pie

The inspiration for this came from my friend Ann who made me a pie using a recipe from the BBC's *Vegetarian Good Food* magazine. I thought the pie was delicious, but have experimented to make a vegan version. This is the result.

serves 6–8

125g/4oz/²/₃ cup couscous

25g/1oz/1 heaped tbsp dried apricots, chopped

25g/1oz/1¹/₂tbsp raisins

300ml/10fl oz/1¹/₄ cups boiling water

3tbsp olive oil

1 onion, chopped

1 clove garlic, crushed (minced)

1tbsp ground coriander

1tbsp ground cinnamon

1 sweet red pepper, deseeded and quartered

1 large aubergine (eggplant), cut lengthwise into 6 slices

350g/12oz frozen puff pastry (flaky pastry), defrosted

3–4 heaped tbsp Cranberry Sauce (page 44)

2 tomatoes, chopped

1tbsp chopped fresh mint

Put the couscous, dried apricots and raisins in a large bowl (you need a large bowl as other ingredients will be added later) and cover with the boiling water. Set aside.

Meanwhile, heat 2 tablespoons of the oil in a saucepan. Add the onion, cover, and cook gently for 10 minutes, until tender. Add the garlic, ground coriander and cinnamon, stir and cook for a further 1–2 minutes, then remove from the heat.

Heat the grill (broiler) to high, and grill (broil) the pepper for 10–15 minutes, until tender and the skin has blackened and blistered in places. Remove the pepper quarters from the heat, cover with a plate and leave them until they are cool enough to handle. Peel off the skin and cut the flesh into 1cm (¹/₂in) dice.

Brush the aubergine (eggplant) on both sides with the remaining oil, place under the grill (broiler), and grill (broil), turning them as necessary, for 6–8 minutes, or until the slices are tender and have browned slightly. Leave them to cool.

Preheat the oven to 230°C/450°F/Gas 8 and place a baking sheet in the centre.

Roll out two-thirds of the pastry and use it to line a 20cm (8in) x 5cm (2in) deep flan tin (tart pan) with a removable base. Spread half the Cranberry Sauce over the base of the pastry.

Add the onion mixture to the couscous, along with the red pepper, tomatoes, mint, parsley, almonds and black olives. Mix well and season with salt and pepper to taste.

Spoon half of the mixture over the Cranberry Sauce, smooth the top, then lay half the aubergine (eggplant) slices over the top. Cover the aubergine (eggplant) with the rest of the couscous mixture, smooth the top, then finish with a layer of the remaining aubergine (eggplant) slices and the rest of the Cranberry Sauce.

Roll out the rest of the pastry to fit the top. Run a trellis cutter over it if you have one, stretch the pastry over the top of the pie to open out the lattice and trim the edges. Otherwise, cut the pastry into strips and arrange these over the top of the pie in a lattice pattern and trim the ends. Brush with a little soya milk, to glaze.

Bake for 10 minutes, then reduce the heat to 170°C/325°F/Gas 3 and bake for a further 40–45 minutes, until the pie is golden and risen.

1tbsp chopped fresh parsley
75g/3oz/1 cup flaked (slivered) almonds, toasted
125g/4oz/generous ¹/2 cup pitted black olives
salt
freshly ground black pepper
soya milk, for glazing

chestnut and red wine pâté en croûte

This is a festive dish which is especially good for Christmas and winter celebrations. I love the piquant flavour of the Horseradish Sauce with it, and some Vegan Gravy (pages 51 and 45).

serves 4–6

2tbsp olive oil
2 onions, chopped
2 cloves garlic, crushed (minced)
50g/2oz/^{2}/$_3$ cup button mushrooms, sliced, optional
1 glass red wine
450g/1lb/2 cups unsweetened chestnut purée or mashed fresh or canned chestnuts
75g/3oz/1^1/$_2$ cups soft fresh white or brown breadcrumbs
salt
freshly ground black pepper
450g/1lb frozen puff pastry (flaky pastry), defrosted
soya milk, to glaze, optional

Preheat the oven to 230°C/450°F/Gas 8. Heat the oil in a medium-large saucepan. Add the onions and fry for about 10 minutes, until soft. Add the garlic and mushrooms, if using, and cook for a further 2–3 minutes. Pour in the wine and let it bubble away for 1–2 minutes, until most of the liquid has evaporated.

Remove the pan from the heat and stir in the chestnuts, breadcrumbs, and salt and pepper to taste. Leave to cool.

Roll out the pastry into 2 strips, the first measuring about 15 x 30cm (6 x 12in), the second 20–23 x 30cm (8–9 x 12in). Put the first strip onto a baking sheet which has been brushed with cold water.

Spoon the chestnut mixture over the pastry, leaving a gap about 1cm (¹/₂in) around the edge. Arrange the filling in the middle of the pastry to form a neat loaf-like shape. Brush the edges of the pastry with cold water, then lay the second piece of pastry on top, easing it over the mixture and aligning the edges, then press down lightly to seal. Trim the edges. Cut the trimmings into decorative shapes, if you wish, and stick them on top of the pastry with water. Make a few small steam holes with a fork or skewer, then brush all over with soya milk, if using.

Bake for 7–8 minutes, then reduce the temperature to 200°C/400°F/Gas 6 and bake for a further 20–25 minutes, until the pastry is golden brown, crisp and flaky. Serve at once.

easy pizza

Making your own pizzas may seem unnecessary now that you can buy them everywhere, but nothing beats a homemade one with its thin, crisp base and luscious topping made with your favourite ingredients. They are much easier to make than you might think and fill your home with the most inviting aroma. Once you have made the dough, it will keep in the fridge for a couple of days or so, or can be frozen in pizza-size amounts for use within 4–6 weeks. Then all you have to do is defrost a chunk of dough, roll it out thinly, top with your chosen ingredients – which can be as simple or as elaborate as you like – and bake for 10–15 minutes.

makes 4 x 30cm (12in) pizza bases

400g/14oz/2³/₄ cups strong brown bread flour
¹/₂tsp salt
1 packet of easy-blend yeast
300ml/15fl oz/scant 2 cups tepid (lukewarm) water
olive oil, for greasing

Put the flour, salt and yeast into a large bowl. Add the water and mix until you have a dough which leaves the sides of the bowl clean. Turn the dough out onto a clean worksurface and knead until it feels smooth and silky. (I often count – it seems to make it easier – and 200 times is about right, which takes around 5 minutes.)

Oil the bowl, return the dough, and turn it in the oil so that it is covered, then stretch a piece of clingfilm (plastic wrap) over the top of the bowl and leave in a warm place until the dough has doubled in size. The dough will take as little as 45 minutes to rise in a warm room or up to 2 hours or more in a cold place, such as overnight in the fridge. You can organize things at this stage to suit you.

When the dough has doubled in size, punch the dough down and let it rise again. It will be quicker this time, but if it is ready before you are, you can punch it down again and put it into the fridge or freezer to use later, if you wish.

If you're proceeding at this point, preheat the oven to 200°C/400°F/Gas 6 and oil 2 large baking sheets. Divide the dough into 4 equal pieces, then roll out each one thinly to form a circle about 30cm (12in) across (alternatively, divide the dough into 8 pieces and make 20cm (8in) circles. Transfer the bases to the prepared baking sheets (or freeze those pieces you do not need at this point).

Put your chosen topping on top (see below for some suggestions) and bake for 15–20 minutes, until the dough has cooked in the centre and the top has browned lightly. The pizzas are wonderful straight from the oven, but are also good served warm or cold.

toppings

giardinara

Roll out the pizza base, then spread tomato sauce (homemade is best, page 47, but a good one from a jar will do or else canned tomatoes, drained, seasoned and chopped), then top with thin slices of onion, frozen or drained canned sweetcorn, thinly sliced sweet green or red pepper and button mushrooms and thin stems of asparagus in season, if liked. Drizzle a little olive oil over the top and bake.

tomato and onion

Spread tomato sauce thinly over the pizza base, as above, then top with thinly sliced mild onion – red onion looks pretty or try Spanish for a sweet, oniony topping – and a few black olives.

sweet red pepper and olive

Brush the top of the pizza with olive oil (or cover with tomato sauce as before) then top with thin slices of sweet red pepper (or red and yellow pepper) and some black and/or green olives.

garlic

Brush the top of the pizza with olive oil, then top with 2–3 finely chopped or thinly sliced garlic cloves. Make 3–4 cuts in the top of the pizza. This pizza is good served as an accompaniment to a thick soup, casserole or salad.

little greek 'pies'

These are good served with drinks, as an appetizer, or as a main course, accompanied by a tomato, black olive and red onion salad, a leafy salad and some Hummus or Tahini Dip (pages 13 and 14). This recipe only uses a small amount of filo pastry, but you can rewrap the rest and keep it in the fridge to use within the following 2–3 weeks. Alternatively, you could use the whole packet of filo and increase the amount of filling to 500g/1lb 2oz/9 cups frozen spinach, 4 onions and 4 tablespoons dill. The "pies" freeze well prior to baking and can be cooked from frozen – just add 5 minutes or so longer to the cooking time.

makes 9

Heat the oil in a saucepan. Add the onion and fry for 10 minutes, until tender but not browned. Add the spinach and cook for a further 3–4 minutes, until tender, then remove from the heat. Add the dill, season to taste and then leave to cool.

Preheat the oven to 200°C/400°F/Gas 6. Lay the sheets of filo pastry on a work surface, the longest edge at the top, then cut to make 3 strips from each piece of filo.

Put a spoonful of the spinach mixture on top of a strip of filo, then fold it down to the left, enclosing the spinach, to form a triangular shape. Then fold the filo to the right, and continue until all the filo has been used – you will have a small, neat triangle. Brush with olive oil and place on a baking sheet. Repeat with the other strips until all the filling has been used up.

Bake the "pies" for 15–20 minutes, until crisp and golden. Either serve immediately or leave to cool on a wire rack. They will keep crisp for a while after they have cooled.

1tbsp olive oil, plus extra for brushing
1 onion, chopped
125g/4oz/1 cup frozen spinach, defrosted
1tbsp chopped fresh dill
salt
freshly ground black pepper
3 sheets filo pastry

pasta dishes

Pasta is a great vegan food just as long as it doesn't contain egg, so take time to read the packet. Pasta and Parmesan go together like bread and butter or strawberries and cream, yet there are plenty of vegan alternatives: chopped fresh herbs, for instance, or crunchy toasted nuts, croûtons of bread or crisply fried onion. Experimenting with pasta dishes which are vegan is fun, and there are many more possibilities than you might think.

spaghetti with sweet red pepper

Bring a large pan of water to the boil, then add the pasta. Stir, then let the pasta boil, uncovered, for 7–10 minutes, until just tender.

Meanwhile, heat a grill (broiler) to high, and grill (broil) the pepper sliced until the skin has blistered and charred in places. Remove the pepper from the grill (broiler), cover with a plate, and leave to continue to cook in their own heat.

Heat the oil in a pan. Add the onions and garlic and cook gently for 10 minutes, until softened.

Drain the pasta, return it to the saucepan, then add the onion, garlic, any oil left in the pan and some salt and pepper.

Peel the skin from the pepper slices – it should come away quite easily – then cut into strips and add to the pasta, together with the black olives and basil, if using. Serve at once.

225g/8oz/2 cups spaghetti
1 large sweet red pepper, deseeded and cut into 8 slices
1tbsp olive oil
1 onion, chopped
1 large clove garlic, crushed (minced)
salt
freshly ground black pepper
a few black olives, optional
1–2tbsp chopped fresh basil, optional

spaghetti with pesto

A simple tomato or tomato, lettuce and onion salad goes well with this light pasta dish.

serves 2

225g/8oz/2 cups spaghetti

for the pesto:
3–4 good sprigs of fresh
basil, stalks removed
1 large clove garlic, crushed
(minced)
50g/2oz/scant $^{1}/_{2}$ cup pine
nuts
4tbsp olive oil
salt
freshly ground black pepper

Bring a large pan of water to the boil, then add the pasta. Stir, then let the pasta boil, uncovered, for 7–10 minutes, until just tender.

Meanwhile, make the pesto. Blend together the basil, garlic and pine nuts until smooth, then gradually add the oil to make a thick sauce.

Drain the pasta, return it to the saucepan with the pesto. Season with salt and pepper to taste and stir with a fork until the pasta is coated in the sauce. Serve at once.

rigatoni with tomato sauce

Rigatoni – the big, ribbed macaroni-type pasta – is particularly good in this recipe because the sauce clings to it well, but other pasta shapes are also good, so use whatever you have to hand.

serves 4

Bring a large pan of water to the boil, then add the pasta. Stir, then let the pasta boil, uncovered, for 7–10 minutes, until just tender.

Meanwhile, if you are using fresh tomatoes, put them in a bowl, cover with boiling water and leave for 1–2 minutes. Drain and peel – the skin should slip off easily with the aid of a pointed knife. Chop the tomatoes roughly. If you are using canned tomatoes, chop them.

Heat 1 tablespoon of the oil in a medium-sized saucepan. Add the onion and fry for 5 minutes, covered. Add the tomatoes and the garlic, stir well, then cover and simmer for 15–20 minutes. Season with salt and pepper to taste.

Drain the pasta, return it to the saucepan with the remaining olive oil and some salt and pepper and stir gently. Put the pasta on warmed plates and pour the sauce on top. If you are using the basil, tear up the leaves and sprinkle them over the top.

225–350g/8–12oz/2^2/3–4 cups rigatoni
450g/1lb/2^1/2 cups fresh tomatoes or 425g/15oz can tomatoes
2tbsp olive oil
1 onion, chopped
1 large clove garlic, crushed (minced)
salt
freshly ground black pepper
sprig of fresh basil, optional

variation

tomato sauce with aubergines (eggplant)

This is particularly good with a green pasta, such as tagliatelle verde. To make, follow the recipe above. Additionally, slice an aubergine (eggplant) thinly lengthwise, then cut the slices into strips about 5cm (2in) long x 2.5cm (1in) wide. Brush them lightly with olive oil and grill (broil) for 6–7 minutes, until tender. Put the pasta on warmed plates, pour the sauce over the top, then pile the aubergine (eggplant) strips on top of the sauce.

penne rigate with artichoke hearts, sun-dried tomatoes, olives and basil

serves 2

Bring a large pan of water to the boil, then add the pasta. Stir, then let the pasta boil, uncovered, for 7–10 minutes, until just tender.

Meanwhile, heat the oil in a large saucepan. Add the onion, cover, and cook gently for 10 minutes, until tender but not browned. Add the garlic, cook for a further 1–2 minutes, then stir in the sun-dried tomatoes and tomatoes, together with their juice, breaking them up with a wooden spoon. Let the mixture simmer for about 10–15 minutes, until the liquid has reduced. Add the artichoke hearts, black olives and a good seasoning of salt and freshly ground black pepper.

Drain the pasta and return it to the still-warm saucepan with some salt. Either stir in the artichoke and tomato sauce, or toss the pasta in a tablespoon of olive oil, then serve it on warmed plates and spoon the sauce over. Tear the basil leaves, if using, and sprinkle over the top.

250g/8oz/2²/₃ cups penne rigate
1tbsp oil from the sun-dried tomatoes
1 onion, chopped
2 cloves garlic, crushed (minced)
8 sun-dried tomatoes in oil, drained and chopped
425g/15oz can tomatoes
225g/8oz canned artichoke hearts, sliced
50g/2oz/¹/₂ cup black olives
salt
freshly ground black pepper
olive oil, for dressing pasta, optional
6 fresh basil leaves, optional

fusilli with courgettes (zucchini) and tomatoes

serves 2

250g/8oz/2²/₃ cups fusilli

2tbsp olive oil, plus extra for dressing pasta, optional

1–2 cloves garlic, crushed (minced)

225g/8oz/2 cups courgettes (zucchini), sliced

225g/8oz/1¹/₂ cups tomatoes, peeled and chopped

salt

freshly ground black pepper

6 large fresh basil leaves, optional

Bring a large pan of water to the boil, then add the pasta. Stir, then let the pasta boil, uncovered, for 7–10 minutes, until just tender.

Meanwhile, heat the oil in a pan or frying pan. Add the garlic and courgettes (zucchini). Cook for 2–3 minutes, stirring often, then add the tomatoes and salt and pepper to taste. Cook for a further 2–3 minutes.

Drain the pasta and return it to the still-warm saucepan with some salt. Either stir in the courgettes (zucchini) and tomato sauce, or toss the pasta in a tablespoon of olive oil, then serve it on warmed plates and spoon the sauce over. Tear the basil leaves, if using, and sprinkle them over the top.

fusilli colbuco with aubergine (eggplant) and wine sauce

Fusilli colbuco, a long, spiral-shaped pasta, is particularly attractive in this dish, but any other long pasta shape, including spaghetti, would be a good alternative.

serves 4

Heat 2 tablespoons of the oil in a medium-sized saucepan. Add the onion and cook for 5 minutes, without browning. Add the aubergine (eggplant), garlic, green pepper, tomatoes and wine and cook gently for 25 minutes, until the vegetables have softened. Season to taste.

Towards the end of the cooking time, cook the pasta. Bring a large pan of water to the boil, add the pasta, stir, then let it boil, uncovered, for 7–10 minutes, until the pasta is just tender.

Drain the pasta and return it to the still-warm saucepan with some salt. Either stir in the aubergine (eggplant) and tomato sauce, or toss the pasta in a tablespoon of olive oil, then serve it on warmed plates and spoon the sauce over. Tear the basil leaves, if using, and sprinkle them on top.

1 onion, chopped
2–3tbsp olive oil
2 medium-sized aubergines (eggplant), about 450g/1lb in total, cut into 3mm/$\frac{1}{8}$in dice
1 clove garlic, crushed (minced)
1 sweet green pepper, deseeded and chopped
225g/8oz/1$\frac{1}{2}$ cups tomatoes, skinned and chopped
4tbsp red or white wine
salt
freshly ground black pepper
a few fresh basil leaves, optional
350g/12oz/4 cups fusilli colbuco pasta

tagliatelle verde with red lentil and tomato sauce

This very hearty, warming pasta dish is a useful standby as it can be made from ingredients most of us tend to have in our storecupboards.

serves 4

1 large onion, chopped

3tbsp olive oil

2 cloves garlic, crushed (minced)

1/2tsp ground cinnamon

225g/8oz/generous cup red lentils, washed

425g/15oz can tomatoes

450ml/3/4 pint/scant 2 cups water

salt

freshly ground black pepper

225–350g/8–12oz/2²/3–4 cups tagliatelle verde

50–125g/2–4 oz/1/2–1 cup grated (shredded) vegan cheese, to serve, optional

Heat 2 tablespoons of the oil in a saucepan. Add the onion and cook for 10 minutes. Add the garlic, cinnamon, lentils, tomatoes and water and bring to the boil. Let the mixture simmer gently for about 20 minutes, until the lentils are tender. Taste and season with salt and pepper.

A little before the end of the cooking time, bring a large pan of water to the boil. Add the pasta, stir, then let the pasta boil, uncovered, for 7–10 minutes, until just tender.

Drain the pasta and return it to the still-warm saucepan with some salt. Either stir in the lentil and tomato sauce, or toss the pasta in the remaining olive oil, then serve it on warmed plates and spoon the sauce over it. Sprinkle the cheese over the top, if using.

variation

tagliatelle verde with lentil and red wine sauce

Make as described above, but replace 75–150ml/3–5fl oz/ scant to generous 1/2 cup – as much as you like – of the water with red wine.

spaghetti with mushroom 'bolognese' sauce

This rich mushroom sauce makes an excellent vegan alternative to the classic Bolognese sauce.

serves 2

Heat 2 tablespoons of the oil in a medium-sized saucepan. Add the onion and fry, covered, for 5 minutes. Add the mushrooms to the onion, together with the garlic, and fry, stirring often, for a further 5 minutes, until browned slightly.

Add the tomatoes, sherry or wine, tomato purée (paste) and basil. Mix well, then cover, and leave the sauce to simmer for 25–30 minutes, until thick and tasty. Season to taste with salt and pepper.

A little before the end of the cooking time, bring a large pan of water to the boil. Add the pasta, stir, then let the pasta boil, uncovered, for 7–10 minutes, until it is just tender.

Drain the pasta and return it to the still-warm saucepan with some salt. Either stir in the sauce, or just toss the pasta in the remaining olive oil, then serve it on warmed plates and spoon the sauce over the top.

3tbsp olive oil
1 onion, very finely chopped
300g/11oz/scant 4 cups mushrooms, washed and finely chopped
1 large clove garlic, crushed (minced)
225g/8oz can tomatoes
2tbsp sherry or 3–4tbsp red wine
4tbsp tomato purée (tomato paste)
1tsp dried basil
1tsp black olive pâté or Tapenade (page 16) or pitted and mashed black olives
salt
freshly ground black pepper
225–350g/8–12oz/1^1/$_2$–2 cups spaghetti

tagliatelle with cream and walnuts

Serve this quick, rich and delicious dish with a green salad.

serves 4

350g/12oz/4 cups tagliatelle	Bring a large pan of water to the boil, then add the pasta. Stir, then let the pasta boil, uncovered, for 7–10 minutes, until just tender.
1tbsp cornflour (cornstarch)	
250ml/8fl oz/1 cup soya cream	Meanwhile, blend the cornflour (cornstarch) with a little of the cream in a heatproof bowl. Put the rest of the cream and the garlic into a small pan and heat to boiling point.
2 cloves garlic, crushed (minced)	
salt	Pour the boiling cream over the cornflour (cornstarch) mixture, stir well, then return the sauce to the pan and stir over a gentle heat for 1–2 minutes, until it has thickened. Season with salt and pepper to taste.
freshly ground black pepper	
50g/2oz/½ cup walnuts, roughly chopped	

Drain the pasta and return it to the still-warm saucepan. Add the cream and garlic sauce and the walnuts and adjust the seasoning to taste, if necessary. Mix well, then serve immediately.

fusilli verde with mushrooms and cream

Heat 2 tablespoons of the olive oil in a saucepan. Add the onion and cook for 10 minutes, until it has softened. Add the garlic and mushrooms and cook for 15–20 minutes, until all the liquid has evaporated.

Stir in the cornflour (cornstarch), cook for 1–2 minutes, then add the soya cream and stir until thickened. Cook gently for 2 minutes, then remove from the heat and season with salt, pepper and freshly grated nutmeg to taste.

A little while before the end of the cooking time, bring a large pan of water to the boil. Add the pasta, stir, then let the pasta boil, uncovered, for 7–10 minutes, until it is just tender.

Drain the pasta and return it to the still-warm saucepan with some salt. Either stir in the mushroom sauce, or just toss the pasta in the remaining olive oil then serve it on warmed plates and spoon the sauce over.

350g/12oz/4 cups fusilli verde
1 onion, chopped
3tbsp olive oil
1 clove garlic, crushed (minced)
350g/12oz/4 cups button mushrooms, wiped and sliced
1tbsp cornflour (cornstarch)
250ml/8fl oz/1 cup soya cream
salt
freshly ground black pepper
freshly grated nutmeg

pasta and broccoli béchamel

serves 2–3

225g/8oz/4 cups broccoli, cut into small florets
100g/4oz/1^{1}/3 cups short macaroni, shells or other pasta shapes
1 quantity Béchamel Sauce (page 49)
salt
freshly ground black pepper
40g/1^{1}/2oz/^{3}/4 cup fresh breadcrumbs and 1tbsp vegan margarine, for topping, optional

Cook the broccoli florets in 1cm (^{1}/2in) of boiling water for 3–4 minutes, until nearly tender. Drain and set aside.

Bring a large pan of water to the boil, then add the pasta and stir. Let the pasta boil, uncovered, for 7–10 minutes, until just tender. Drain the pasta.

Meanwhile, gently heat the Béchamel Sauce. Add the pasta and broccoli, then stir gently over the heat until heated through.

Either serve straight away or pour the mixture into a shallow heatproof dish. Top with the breadcrumbs and dot with the margarine and cook under a hot grill (broiler) until the top has become golden brown and crisp.

spinach lasagne

This makes a substantial, tasty lasagne – great for feeding a crowd, especially if accompanied by a crisp green salad with fresh herbs and some robust red wine.

serves 6

Preheat the oven to 200°C/400°F/Gas 6.

Heat the oil in a large saucepan. Add the onion and fry for 10 minutes, until it has softened but not browned. Add the garlic and cook for a moment or two, then remove the pan from the heat. Add the spinach and salt, pepper and nutmeg to taste.

To assemble the lasagne, rinse the lasagne sheets under cold running water. Lay enough sheets over the base of a greased, large, rectangular baking dish to cover it. Spoon a little of the White Sauce to thinly coat the lasagne. Spread half the spinach mixture on top, then half the Tomato Sauce, then another layer of lasagne and some more White Sauce. Follow with the rest of the spinach, the remaining Tomato Sauce, a layer of lasagne and the rest of the White Sauce.

Bake for about 35 minutes, until the lasagne is tender and the top has become golden brown.

1 tbsp olive oil
1 large onion, chopped
2 cloves garlic, crushed (minced)
900g/2lb/16 cups fresh or frozen spinach, cooked and drained
salt
freshly ground black pepper
freshly grated nutmeg
150–175g/5–6oz ready-to-use lasagne sheets
1 quantity Tomato Sauce (page 47)
2 × quantity White Sauce (page 48)

lasagne al forno

This does take a bit of time to make, but it can be made well in advance, ready for baking, and is an excellent way of feeding a crowd, so it is worth the effort.

serves 8

225–350g/8–12oz ready-to-use lasagne verde sheets

for the mushroom sauce:
2tbsp olive oil
1 onion, very finely chopped
300g/11oz/scant 4 cups mushrooms, washed and finely chopped
1 large clove garlic, crushed (minced)
225g/8oz can tomatoes
2tbsp sherry or 3–4 tbsp red wine
4 heaped tbsp tomato purée (paste)
1tsp dried basil
1tsp black olive pâté or Tapenade (page 16) or pitted and mashed black olives

First, make the mushroom sauce. Heat the oil in a medium-sized saucepan. Add the onion and fry for 5 minutes, covered. Add the mushrooms, together with the garlic, and fry, stirring often, for a further 5 minutes, until browned slightly. Add the tomatoes, sherry or wine, tomato purée (paste) and basil. Mix well, then cover and leave to simmer for 25–30 minutes, until thickened.

Meanwhile, make the cream sauce. Melt the margarine in a medium-sized saucepan, then add the flour. Stir over the heat for a moment, then stir in a third of the soya milk. Continue to stir until the milk has been incorporated and the mixture has thickened, then stir in another third of the milk and stir again. Repeat with the final third, stirring until the sauce is smooth. Leave the sauce to cook over a very gentle heat for 10 minutes, then remove from the heat and stir in the cream, a good grating of nutmeg and salt and pepper to taste.

To assemble the lasagne, first grease a dish thoroughly. Rinse the lasagne sheets under cold running water, then arrange in the base of the prepared dish to cover the bottom. On top of this add half the mushroom sauce, then a third of the cream sauce, smoothing them evenly. Top this with another layer of lasagne, then the rest of the mushroom sauce followed by another third of the cream sauce. Finish with a layer of lasagne, followed by the remainder of the cream sauce.

The dish can now be kept until you are ready to bake it. To cook, preheat the oven to 180°C/350°F/Gas 4 and bake for about 35 minutes.

for the cream sauce:
50g/2oz/4tbsp vegan margarine
50g/2oz/scant $^1/_2$ cup plain (all-purpose) flour
750ml/1$^1/_4$ pints/3 cups soya milk
250ml/8fl oz/1 cup soya cream
freshly grated nutmeg
salt
freshly ground black pepper

You can use canned or dried beans and lentils for the recipes in this section. The advantage of dried beans is that they're cheaper and also you know what you're getting in terms of salt and other additives. I'm finding that I'm now more likely to use the dried ones for these reasons, and because of the fact that they're more ecologically sound – no can to manufacture and then dispose of.

It's useful to know that 100g/3^1/$_2$oz/^{1}/$_2$ cup of dried beans or lentils, when cooked, is equivalent to a 425g/15oz can. So, if you soak and cook a 500g/1lb 2 oz bag of dried beans or lentils then divide it into 5 equal portions for freezing, then each portion can be used in place of a 425g/15oz can.

How to prepare dried beans

Pick out and discard any really shrivelled beans or pieces of grit and rinse them well under cold running water. Put the beans in a large saucepan and cover with their height again of cold water. Leave to soak overnight (they need to soak for 8 hours). Alternatively, bring them to the boil, simmer for 2 minutes, then remove from the heat, cover, and leave to stand for 1 hour.

After soaking (or pre-cooking) the beans, drain and rinse them, cover with as much fresh water as before and bring to the boil. Boil them vigorously for 10 minutes (this is a good idea for all beans but vital when cooking soya or red kidney beans as the heat destroys any toxins they may contain), then reduce the heat so that they simmer steadily until tender. This usually takes from 50 minutes to $1^{1}/_{2}$ hours, although chickpeas (garbanzos) can be obstinate and may take 2 hours or so to become soft. If your beans take a long time to become tender, this usually means that they are rather old. They do not keep for ever, so buy them from a shop with a rapid turnover, and use them within a few months. Also, do not add salt until the beans are cooked – if you add it during cooking, it makes the beans tough.

How to prepare black-eyed beans, split peas and lentils

Black-eyed beans, split peas and lentils of all types do not need to be soaked before cooking (though they can be soaked if you want to reduce the cooking time by a few minutes).

Put them in a large pan, cover with their height again of cold water and bring to the boil. Leave to simmer until tender. Red split lentils take about 20 minutes, while black-eyed beans and other types of lentils take about 35–45 minutes.

felafel

This is a traditional Israeli recipe for the crisp, tasty rissoles. You might find it is worth making double the quantity of felafel (using a 500g/1lb 2 oz pack of dried chickpeas/ garbanzos), as I do, and freezing them. They then only need to be reheated under the grill (broiler) or in a microwave, and make useful quick snacks served with salad, Hummus (page 13), pitta bread and Tahini Dip (page 14). You need a food processor with a good sharp blade to make this – then it's surprisingly easy.

makes about 22

250g/9oz/1^{1}/3 cups dried chickpeas (garbanzos)
25g/1oz/^{1}/2 cup fresh parsley, thick stalks removed
1 clove garlic, roughly sliced
1 onion, roughly chopped
1tsp ground coriander
1tsp ground cumin
1tsp sea salt
oil, for deep-frying

Put the chickpeas (garbanzos) into a large bowl and cover generously with cold water. Leave to soak for 24 hours. Drain and rinse the chickpeas (garbanzos). Put them in a food processor, together with the parsley, garlic, onion, spices and salt. Blend to a grainy paste which holds together – if it's on the wet side, chill in the fridge for an hour or so.

Heat the oil until it forms bubbles around the end of a chopstick when dipped into it. Form the mixture into walnut-sized balls, then flatten them slightly. Place them in the oil, 3 or 4 at a time, and fry for 2–3 minutes, until crisp and brown on the outside, then drain on kitchen paper.

Serve the felafel immediately or freeze them. To freeze, put the cooled felafel on a tray and put them in the freezer until firm, then transfer them to a polythene bag or container. To serve, microwave or grill (broil) them straight from the freezer.

spicy beanburgers

These are easy to make, freeze well and can be cooked from frozen. They're good in burger buns with tomato ketchup, lettuce, sliced tomatoes and onions, Vegan Mayonnaise (page 30), or whatever you fancy.

(page 30)

makes 8

Preheat the oven to 200°C/400°F/gas 6. Heat the oil in a large saucepan. Add the onion and stir, cover, and cook over a moderate heat for 5 minutes, stirring occasionally. Add the carrot, green pepper and garlic and cook for a further 5 minutes. Add the spices, stir for 1–2 minutes, then remove the pan from the heat.

Mash the beans and add to the onion mixture, together with the fresh breadcrumbs and season to taste.

Divide the mixture into 8 equal pieces, then form each one into burgers and coat with the dried breadcrumbs. (If you want to freeze them, do so at this stage: put them on a tray in the freezer and freeze until they are firm. Transfer them to a polythene bag or container.)

To cook the fresh or frozen burgers, place them on an oiled baking sheet and bake for 15–20 minutes for freshly made ones, or 10 minutes longer for frozen ones, until brown and crisp on one side. Turn the burgers over and cook the other side for 10–15 minutes for freshly made ones, 5 minutes longer for frozen ones. Drain on absorbent kitchen paper and then serve hot or warm.

1tbsp olive oil, plus extra as required

1 onion, chopped

1 carrot, finely chopped or grated

$^1/_2$ sweet green pepper, deseeded and chopped

1 clove garlic, crushed (minced)

$^1/_4$–$^1/_2$tsp hot chilli powder, optional

1tsp ground coriander

2 x 425g/15oz can kidney beans, drained

50g/2oz/1 cup fresh wholewheat breadcrumbs

salt

freshly ground black pepper

100g/4oz/1 cup dried wholewheat breadcrumbs, for coating

onion bhajis

Bhajis make a delicious snack or even a filling meal when served with some plainly cooked rice, chutney and perhaps a salad or raita (chopped cucumber or fresh herbs mixed into natural, vegan yogurt).

serves 2

oil, for deep-frying
125g/4oz/scant cup gram or
chickpea (garbanzo) flour
2tsp ground coriander
1tsp ground cumin
pinch of cayenne
salt
freshly ground black pepper
150ml/¼ pint/⅔ cup
lukewarm water
1 onion, finely chopped
1tbsp chopped fresh
coriander (cilantro),
optional

Sift the chickpea (garbanzo) flour into a bowl with the ground coriander, cumin and cayenne. Add a teaspoon of salt, then pour in the water, stirring, to make a batter. Stir the onion and coriander (cilantro), if using, into the batter.

Heat enough oil in a saucepan for deep-frying – it is ready when bubbles form immediately around the handle of a wooden spoon when dipped into it. Place heaped teaspoons of the mixture into the oil and fry them for about 5 minutes, until they are really crisp and the onion is cooked.

Drain the bhajis on absorbent kitchen paper and keep the first batch warm, uncovered, while you cook the rest. Then serve immediately.

dal

Delicious, fat-free and really simple to make, this makes a complete main course if served with steamed brown rice and a salad of chopped tomatoes and spring onions (scallions).

serves 4

Wash and drain the lentils, picking out any damaged ones or pieces of grit, then put them in a saucepan with the onion and water. Bring to the boil, then remove the froth which forms on the top.

Add the ginger and turmeric to the lentils and leave to simmer gently for 30–40 minutes, until the lentils are very soft. Stir towards the end of the cooking time to prevent the lentils sticking.

Dry-roast the cumin and coriander seeds by stirring in a small pan for a few seconds until they release their spicy aroma, then add to the lentil mixture. Add the chilli powder, if using, lemon juice, salt and pepper to taste.

Serve sprinkled with chopped fresh coriander (cilantro), if using. This is especially good made in advance and then reheated, which allows the flavours time to develop.

200 /7oz/1 cup dried red split lentils
1 onion, sliced
1 litre/1^{3}/4 pints/4 cups water
2 thin slices of fresh ginger root
^{1}/2tsp turmeric
1tsp cumin seeds
1tsp coriander seeds
pinch of chilli powder
squeeze of lemon juice
salt
freshly ground black pepper
1tbsp chopped fresh coriander (cilantro), optional

mixed vegetable dal

A more elaborate dal than the recipe on page 101, but still quick and easy to make. It serves 2–4 people depending on what you serve with it – Indian breads and/or boiled rice and maybe some chutney are fine accompaniments. Any left over dal is good, if not better, the next day. Again, the recipe is fat-free, so for this reason it is a special favourite of mine, as well as for its flavour and comforting qualities.

serves 2–4

200g/7oz/1 cup dried red split lentils

2 thin slices of fresh root ginger

$\frac{1}{2}$tsp turmeric

1tsp cumin seeds

1tsp ground coriander

pinch of chilli powder

1 litre/1$\frac{3}{4}$ pints/4 cups water

1 onion, sliced

2 carrots, scraped and sliced

1 clove garlic, crushed (minced)

125g/4oz/scant cup frozen peas

juice of $\frac{1}{2}$ lemon

salt

freshly ground black pepper

Put the lentils, ginger, turmeric, cumin seeds, ground coriander (cilantro) and chilli powder into a medium-sized saucepan with the water and bring to the boil.

Add the onion, carrots and garlic to the lentil mixture. The lentil mixture needs to simmer for about 25 minutes. At first it will look hopelessly watery, then it will become thick and soft, like porridge. It's ready when the vegetables are tender.

Add the peas and cook for a further 2–3 minutes, until they are heated through. Stir in the lemon juice and season to taste with salt and freshly ground black pepper.

lentil burgers

This recipe makes a lot of burgers but they do freeze well. Simply freeze them before cooking and then, when you want to use them, cook them from frozen, allowing 10–15 minutes longer than stated in the recipe. Alternatively, the recipe can be halved. Serve the burgers in buns or with a sauce and vegetables or salad.

makes 16

Wash and drain the lentils, picking out any damaged ones or pieces of grit, then put them into a saucepan with the water. Bring to the boil, cover, and cook the lentils very gently for 20–25 minutes, until they are soft and pale and all the water has been absorbed.

Preheat the oven to 200°C/400°F/Gas 6.

Heat the oil in a saucepan. Add the onion and fry for 10 minutes, until it is tender and has browned lightly. Just before the onion is ready, add the thyme and oregano and cook for a minute or two longer.

Boil the potatoes until tender, then mash them. Add the lentils to the potatoes, along with the onion, grated nutmeg to taste, parsley and salt and freshly ground black pepper.

Form the mixture into burgers and coat with flour. Brush a baking sheet with olive oil and heat it in the preheated oven for 5 minutes. Place the burgers on the baking sheet and bake for 15–20 minutes, until browned on one side, then turn them over and bake for a further 10–15 minutes, until browned.

350g/12oz/1¾ cups dried red split lentils
400ml/¾ pint/scant 2 cups water
1tbsp olive oil, plus extra for greasing
1 large onion, chopped
1tsp dried thyme
1tsp dried oregano
450g/1lb/3 cups potatoes, peeled and cut into even-sized pieces
freshly grated nutmeg
2tbsp chopped fresh parsley
salt
freshly ground black pepper
flour, for coating

lentil loaf

This is one of the simplest recipes for lentil loaf I know, and it is a particular favourite with my family, so I couldn't leave it out. It's good either hot or cold, with lightly cooked vegetables and a savoury sauce or with a crisp salad.

serves 4–6

500g/1lb 2oz/2^1/2 cups dried red split lentils
600ml/1 pint/2^1/2 cups water
2tbsp olive oil
2 large onions, finely chopped
1tsp dried mixed herbs or sage
1tbsp lemon juice
salt
freshly ground black pepper
3–4tbsp wholewheat flour or dried breadcrumbs, to coat
a little soya oil, for greasing

Wash and drain the lentils, picking out any damaged ones or pieces of grit, then put them into a saucepan with the water, bring to the boil, then turn the heat right down.

Cover, and cook for 20–25 minutes, until the lentils are soft, pale-coloured and all the water has been absorbed. Keep an eye on the lentils towards the end of the cooking time as they may stick, but they need to be dry, so only add a very little extra water, if any.

Meanwhile, heat the oil in a large saucepan and fry the onion, covered, over a fairly gentle heat for 10 minutes.

Preheat the oven to 190°C/375°F/Gas 5. Mix together the lentils, onions, herbs, lemon juice and season to taste. Form the mixture into a loaf shape, coating it with wholewheat flour or breadcrumbs.

Pour some oil into a roasting tin – enough to coat the base thinly – then heat it in the preheated oven. When the oil is very hot, place the lentil loaf in the middle of the tin and spoon a little of the oil over it. Bake for about 45 minutes, or until it has browned and is crisp all over. Baste – spooning some of the oil over the loaf – every 15 minutes or so, if possible. When it is ready, lift it out of the tin and place on a warmed serving dish. Serve in thick slices.

refried red beans

This simple dish is good with tortilla chips, a crisp green salad and Guacamole (page 15), or slices of ripe avocado.

serves 4

If using dried beans, soak and cook them as described on page 97. Heat the oil in a large saucepan. Add the onion, cover, then cook, stirring occasionally, over a moderate heat for 8 minutes. Add the garlic and chilli, then cook for 2 minutes.

Meanwhile, drain the canned beans, if using, and mash roughly with a fork, so the texture is chunky. Add the beans to the onion mixture with the tomatoes. Cook gently, stirring, until heated through.

Season to taste and snip the coriander (cilantro), if using, over the top to garnish before serving.

2 × 425g/15oz cans red
kidney beans, drained, or
200g/7oz/generous cup
dried red kidney beans
2tbsp olive oil
2 onions, chopped
2 cloves garlic, crushed
(minced)
1 green chilli, deseeded and
finely chopped
2 tomatoes, skinned and
chopped
salt
freshly ground black pepper
fresh coriander (cilantro),
to garnish, optional

tofu and mushroom scramble

This is rather like a non-dairy version of scrambled eggs with mushrooms. It's good on its own or served with fingers of hot, crisp toast.

serves 2

1tbsp olive oil
225g/8oz/2 cups button mushrooms, wiped and sliced
1 packet silken tofu, undrained
pinch of turmeric
1tbsp tamari
freshly ground black pepper
chopped fresh parsley, to garnish, optional

Heat the oil in a saucepan and fry the mushrooms for 2–3 minutes, until they are starting to become tender. Add the undrained tofu, turmeric (this gives the dish a lovely colour) and tamari.

Mix well while heating through, until the tofu becomes scrambled. Season with freshly ground black pepper and serve immediately, sprinkled with fresh parsley, if using.

quick and easy red bean chilli

This quick chilli can be served with bread, or mashed or baked potatoes, or pasta or rice. If there's some left over, it's also good cold with a salad or stuffed into pitta bread or as a filling for tortillas.

serves 2

If using dried beans, soak and cook them as described on page 97. Heat the oil in a medium-large saucepan. Add the onion, cover, and cook for 5 minutes. Add the garlic, red pepper and carrot, stir, then cover and cook for 10 minutes.

Stir the tomatoes into the mixture, breaking them up with a spoon. Add the red chilli or chilli powder, to taste – start with ¼ teaspoon, adding more depending on how hot you want the mixture to be. Cook gently, uncovered, for 10–15 minutes, until the carrots are tender.

Add the red kidney beans and cook for a further 1–2 minutes to heat through. Season with salt and pepper to taste, and add a bit more chilli powder if you would like more of a kick, then serve.

1tbsp olive oil
1 onion, chopped
1 clove garlic, crushed (minced)
1 sweet red pepper, deseeded and chopped
1 carrot, scraped and diced
425g/15oz can tomatoes
1 dried red chilli, crumbled, or chilli powder, to taste
425g/15oz can red kidney beans, drained, or
100g/3¹/₂oz/ generous ¹/₂ cup dried red kidney beans
salt
freshly ground black pepper

green lentil chilli burgers with creamy dill sauce

This is a pleasant combination of hot and cool, crisp and creamy. Serve it with a simple salad, such as tomato or lettuce and tomato, or steamed vegetables, such as broccoli. The burgers are best deep-fried, which you can do in a medium saucepan rather than going through the rigmarole of using a deep-fryer, or they can be shallow-fried.

serves 3–4
(makes 8–9)

1tsp olive oil
1 onion, chopped
1 clove garlic, crushed
(minced)
1 green chilli, deseeded and
chopped or chilli powder,
to taste
1tbsp ground coriander
oil, for deep- or shallow-
frying
425g/15oz can green
lentils, drained, or
100 g/3$\frac{1}{2}$ oz/
$\frac{1}{2}$ cup dried green lentils,
6–8 sprigs of fresh
coriander (cilantro)
50g/2oz/1 cup soft, fresh
wholewheat breadcrumbs
salt
freshly ground black pepper

If using dried lentils, soak and cook them as described on page 97. Heat the oil in a saucepan. Add the onion and fry, covered, for 5 minutes, until it starts to soften. Add the garlic, chilli and ground coriander, cover, and fry for a further 2–3 minutes, then remove from the heat.

Put the lentils in a food processor with the onion and spice mixture and the fresh coriander (cilantro). Process until it forms a thick purée. Alternatively, mash the lentils and onion mixture thoroughly with a potato masher until it holds together. Chop the coriander (cilantro) and add it at the end.

Put the purée into a bowl and stir in the soft bread-crumbs until the mixture holds together, but do not allow the mixture to become stiff. Set aside for 5–10 minutes to allow the breadcrumbs to swell, then add a few more if necessary. Season with salt and pepper to taste.

Divide the mixture into 8–9 equal portions, then form into balls or burger shapes. Mix the arrowroot with 3 tablespoons of cold water. Dip the burgers first into the arrowroot mixture, then into the dried breadcrumbs, making sure they are well coated.

Heat the oil for deep or shallow frying, then fry the burgers until they are crisp, brown and heated through. Drain well on kitchen paper.

Stir the fresh dill into the Mustard Cream Dressing and serve with the burgers.

for the coating:
3tbsp arrowroot
about 4tbsp dried
wholewheat breadcrumbs

for the sauce:
2tbsp chopped fresh dill
1 quantity Mustard Cream
Dressing (page 31)

chickpea (garbanzo) purée with spicy onion topping

Deliciously simple, this is good with some warm bread and, perhaps, a cucumber and tomato salad with some chopped fresh coriander (cilantro) and slices of lemon.

serves 2

425g/15oz can chickpeas (garbanzos) or 100g/3^{1}/2oz/generous ^{1}/2 cup dried chickpeas (garbanzos)

2tbsp olive oil

2 onions, chopped

2 cloves garlic, crushed (minced)

2tsp ground coriander

1tsp ground cumin

salt

freshly ground black pepper

If using dried chickpeas (garbanzos), soak and cook them as described on page 97, reserving about 150ml/5fl oz/generous ^{1}/2 cup of the cooking liquid. Drain the canned chickpeas (garbanzos), reserving the liquid.

Heat the oil in a saucepan. Add the onions and fry, covered, for 5 minutes, until they start to soften, then add the garlic, coriander and cumin. Cover, and fry for a further 2–3 minutes. Take a third of the mixture and put it into a food processor; continue to gently cook the rest of the onions and spices (don't have the heat too high because the spices must not burn) until the onions have browned.

Add the chickpeas (garbanzos) to the food processor with the onions and about half of the reserved liquid. Whizz to a purée, adding more of the liquid as necessary to make a thick but creamy purée. Season with salt and pepper, then transfer the purée to a saucepan and heat through.

Serve the purée on warmed plates and spoon the remaining crispy, spicy onion mixture on top.

brown lentil bake

I like this bake with cooked vegetables and some homemade Cranberry Sauce and Vegan Gravy (pages 44 and 45) for a warming meal on a chilly day. It's also good served cold, sliced, with salad.

serves 4

Preheat the oven to 180°C/350°F/Gas 4. Heat the oil in a large saucepan. Add the onions and fry for 10 minutes, stirring from time to time, until they have softened and browned lightly.

Add the garlic, lentils, parsley, mixed herbs and soy sauce. Mash by hand or purée briefly in a food processor or blender, until the mixture holds together. Season to taste with salt and pepper, transfer the mixture to a shallow heatproof dish and smooth the top.

Toss the breadcrumbs in a little oil to coat them, then sprinkle over the top of the lentil mixture. Bake for 30–35 minutes, until the crumb topping has browned and is crisp.

2tbsp olive oil, plus a little extra for topping
2 large onions, finely chopped
1 large clove garlic, crushed (minced)
225g/8oz/generous cup dried green or brown lentils, cooked until tender and well drained (page 97)
2tbsp chopped fresh parsley
1tsp dried mixed herbs
2tbsp soy sauce
salt
freshly ground black pepper
25–50g/1–2oz/^{1}/2–1 cup fresh wholewheat breadcrumbs

spiced red lentils and potatoes with caramelized onions

This dish evolved from the rather unpromising starting point of some dried lentils and potatoes. Serve it with a side salad, a spoonful of chutney and perhaps some poppadums for a crunchy contrast. Although this recipe makes enough for just 2 people, to feed 4 double everything, except the oil.

serves 2

125g/4oz/generous $^{1}/_{2}$ cup dried red split lentils

400ml/$^{3}/_{4}$ pint/scant 2 cups water

250g/8oz/1$^{1}/_{2}$ cups potatoes, cut into 2.5cm/1in dice

1–2tbsp oil

2 onions, chopped

1 clove garlic, crushed (minced)

$^{1}/_{2}$tsp turmeric

$^{1}/_{2}$tsp black mustard seeds

$^{1}/_{2}$tsp grated (minced) fresh root ginger

15g/$^{1}/_{2}$oz/1tbsp creamed coconut

Wash and drain the lentils, picking out any damaged ones or pieces of grit, then put them into a saucepan with the water. Bring to the boil, then reduce the heat and simmer gently, uncovered, for 10 minutes.

Add the potatoes and cook for a further 10–15 minutes, until the potatoes are tender and the lentils are soft, pale-coloured and all the water has been absorbed. Keep an eye on the lentils towards the end of the cooking time as they may stick, but since they need to be dry, only add a little extra water. Remove from the heat.

Meanwhile, heat 1 tablespoon of the oil in a pan. Add the onion and fry, covered, for 5 minutes. Put half the onion in a bowl and set aside. Add the garlic, turmeric, mustard seeds and ginger to the remaining onion in the pan, stir, cover, and cook for a further 4–5 minutes.

Add the spiced onion mixture and the creamed coconut to the lentil and potato mixture and stir gently until combined. Add the lemon juice, coriander (cilantro) and season well with salt and pepper, then keep warm.

Return the reserved onion to the saucepan, adding a drop more oil, if necessary, and fry over a moderate-high heat for 3–5 minutes, until golden brown and crisp. Serve the lentil mixture with the crispy caramelized onions spooned over the top.

squeeze of lemon juice
$1/2$ packet fresh coriander
(cilantro), chopped
salt
freshly ground black pepper

white beans in cream

This rich and delicious dish is lovely for a treat, served with fingers of toast and a crisp green salad.

serves 2

1tbsp olive oil
1 onion, chopped
1 clove garlic, crushed (minced)
250ml/8fl oz/1 cup soya cream
425g/15oz can white beans (haricot/navy, cannellini or butter/lima beans), drained, or 100g/3^{1}/2oz/^{1}/2 cup dried white beans
squeeze of lemon juice
salt
freshly ground black pepper
freshly grated nutmeg
chopped fresh parsley, to garnish, optional

If using dried beans, soak and cook them as described on page 97. Heat the oil in a medium-sized saucepan. Add the onion, cover, and cook gently for 5 minutes, until tender but not browned. Add the garlic and cook for a further 1–2 minutes.

Stir in the cream and leave the mixture to simmer gently for about 5 minutes, until the cream has reduced and thickened. Add the beans and heat gently, stirring often.

Add the lemon juice and season with salt, pepper and freshly grated nutmeg, to taste. Make sure the sauce is really hot, then serve on warmed plates, sprinkled with a little parsley, if using.

variation

white beans and mushrooms in cream

Add 225g/8oz/2^{2}/3 cups sliced white mushrooms to the onion after it has cooked for 5 minutes. Cook for a few more minutes until any liquid produced by the mushrooms has evaporated, then add the cream and continue as described above.

roasted tofu with satay sauce

This is a really delicious and easy way to serve tofu. It is good accompanied by rice and an oriental-style salad or steamed carrots, cut on the diagonal to make oval slices, or mangetout. You need to allow 2 hours for the tofu to marinate.

serves 2

Put the tofu in a shallow bowl. Mix together the ingredients for the marinade and pour it over the tofu, stir gently, then leave for at least 2 hours.

Preheat the oven to 200°C/400°F/Gas 6. Drain the tofu, reserving the marinade. Put the tofu on a lightly oiled baking sheet, in a single layer, and roast in the top of the preheated oven for 25–30 minutes, until browned and fairly crisp.

Meanwhile make the satay sauce: put the peanut butter into a small saucepan with the reserved marinade and the water and heat gently, stirring, until smooth. Stir in the creamed coconut and season with salt. Serve with the warm tofu.

285g/10oz packet firm tofu, drained and cubed

for the marinade:
1 clove garlic, crushed (minced)
2tbsp soy sauce
2tbsp medium or sweet sherry
1tbsp rice vinegar or white wine vinegar

for the satay sauce:
2 slightly rounded tbsp smooth peanut butter
150ml/5fl oz/generous $^1\!/_2$ cup water
2 cloves garlic, crushed (minced)
25g/1oz/2tbsp creamed coconut, cut into pieces
salt

Grains are wonderfully versatile and a health-giving source of protein, complex carbohydrates, fibre, vitamins and minerals – not fattening extras as was once thought.

Think of a grain you would like to have as a main course and plan a meal around it. Brown rice is a healthy basic – a cliché, I know, and with good reason as the more you eat it, the more you love it – but there are others, too. Couscous, which is made from wheat, bulgur wheat and polenta, for example, are all delicious and easy to use and you'll find recipes using them here.

Nuts are higher in protein than grains and a natural partner, so I have also used them in some of the grain dishes as well including a couple of nutty main dishes.

mixed rice with nuts and apricots

This can be served as a warm pilaf or cold salad. Either way, Tomato, Red Onion and Black Olive Salad goes well with it (page 35), as does a lightly dressed mixed leaf salad.

serves 4

Cook the brown and wild rice together in plenty of boiling water, uncovered, for 45 minutes, until they are both tender. Add more boiling water during cooking, if necessary. Drain and rinse under cold running water.

Rinse the basmati rice under cold running water until the water runs clear. Cook it, uncovered, in plenty of boiling water for 10 minutes, or until tender. Drain and rinse as for the brown and wild rice.

Heat the oil in a saucepan. Add the onion, cover, and cook gently for 8–10 minutes, until softened. Add the garlic and cook for a further 1–2 minutes. Mix in the nuts, seeds and apricots, then remove from the heat.

Put the rice – brown, wild and basmati – into a large bowl. Add the onion mixture and the coriander (cilantro), plus the vinaigrette if you are serving it cold; mix well. Season with salt and freshly ground black pepper to taste.

If you are serving the rice hot, put it into a heatproof dish and warm through in an oven preheated to 150°C/300°F/ Gas 2 for 20–30 minutes.

125g/4oz/generous $^1/_2$ cup brown rice

50g/2oz/generous $^1/_4$ cup wild rice

125g/4oz/generous $^1/_2$ cup white basmati rice

2tbsp olive oil

1 onion, chopped

3 cloves garlic, crushed (minced)

125g/4oz/1 cup flaked (slivered) almonds, toasted

25g/1oz/2$^1/_2$tbsp pine nuts

25g/1oz/$^1/_4$ cup pistachio nuts, chopped

1tbsp poppy seeds

50g/2oz/scant $^1/_3$ cup dried apricots, chopped

3tbsp chopped fresh coriander (cilantro) leaves

2–3tbsp vinaigrette, if serving cold

stir-fried chinese vegetables with steamed rice

Start to cook the rice about 40 minutes before you stir-fry the vegetables, since they cook very quickly. The vegetables can be prepared ahead, too, ready for stir-frying. A crushed (minced) garlic clove and about $^1/_2$–1 teaspoon fresh grated (minced) root ginger can be added to this recipe, if you like – add them with the sweetcorn, mushrooms, water chestnuts and bamboo shoots.

serves 2

175g/6oz/scant cup brown rice, washed

salt

350ml/12fl oz/1$^1/_2$ cups water

2tbsp olive oil

200g/7oz packet firm tofu, drained and cubed

1 onion, sliced

2 carrots, scraped and sliced diagonally

125g/4oz/1 cup baby sweetcorn, halved, if large

First, cook the rice: put the rice into a heavy-based saucepan with a tight-fitting lid and sprinkle with a little salt, if you like. Add the water, bring to the boil, cover, and cook over a very low heat for 45 minutes, until the rice is tender and the water has been absorbed.

Meanwhile, about 20 minutes before the rice is ready, heat the oil in a frying pan and fry the tofu cubes until golden, turning them frequently so they brown evenly. Remove the tofu using a slotted spoon and drain on absorbent kitchen paper.

Add the onion and carrots to the frying pan and fry for 5–10 minutes, until they are just beginning to soften. Add the sweetcorn, mushrooms, water chestnuts and bamboo shoots and cook for a further 1–2 minutes to heat through.

Meanwhile, blend the cornflour (cornstarch) with the soy sauce or tamari, then, when the vegetables are ready, add the mixture to the pan, stirring. Add the tofu and stir gently until heated through. Serve immediately.

125g/4oz/1 cup baby button mushrooms, wiped
150g/5oz can water chestnuts, drained
150g/5oz can bamboo shoots, drained
1tsp cornflour (cornstarch)
2tbsp soy sauce or tamari

lemony vegetables and brown rice

This attractive combination of vegetables and brown rice makes a delicious meal. Don't let the long list of ingredients put you off – it's really very simple to make. Once the vegetables have been prepared – and this can be done in advance – the dish does not take long to cook.

serves 4

350g/12oz/1³/₄ cups brown rice, washed
salt
900ml/1¹/₂ pints/3³/₄ cups water
450g/1lb broccoli, cut into florets and stalks cut into matchsticks
225g/8oz/2²/₃ cups mangetout, topped and tailed
1 leek, washed and trimmed
several parsley stalks
few sprigs of fresh thyme
75ml/3fl oz/scant ¹/₂ cup olive oil
75ml/3fl oz/scant ¹/₂ cup water
zest of 1 lemon, thinly sliced
10 carrots, scraped and cut lengthwise into quarters

First, cook the rice: put the rice into a heavy-based saucepan with a tight-fitting lid and sprinkle with a little salt, if you like. Add the water, bring to the boil, cover, and cook over a very low heat for 45 minutes, until the rice is tender and the water has been absorbed.

Meanwhile, bring another large saucepan of water to the boil. Add the broccoli matchsticks to the saucepan and boil for 3–4 minutes, then add the broccoli florets and boil for a further minute. Remove the broccoli with a slotted spoon and place it in a colander under cold running water, to cool. Transfer to a large sieve and set aside to drain thoroughly.

Bring the pan of water back to the boil, then add the mangetout and boil for 1 minute. Transfer them to a colander using a slotted spoon and cool under cold running water as for the broccoli. Place in the colander to drain.

Make a cut down the side of the leek without slicing it in half, then push the parsley stalks and thyme sprigs into the leek and bind with some kitchen string to keep them in place. Put the leek bouquet garni into a saucepan large enough to hold all the vegetables (I use my pressure cooker pan). Add the oil, water and lemon zest and bring to the boil.

Add the carrots, half cover the pan, and simmer for 4 minutes. Remove the pan from the heat and set aside until you want to complete the dish.

About 5 minutes before you want to eat, bring the carrot mixture back to the boil, then add all the remaining vegetables and the garlic. Cook over a high heat, stirring frequently, for about 5 minutes, until the vegetables are just tender. Season with salt and pepper and then serve in a warmed large, shallow casserole dish. Sprinkle the parsley, if using, over the top just before serving. Serve with the rice.

450g/1lb/4 cups button mushrooms, wiped, larger ones halved or quartered
4 large sweet red peppers, deseeded and cut into strips
2 bunches of spring onions (scallions), topped, tailed and trimmed
6 large cloves garlic, crushed (minced) or finely chopped
freshly ground black pepper
2tbsp chopped fresh parsley, to garnish, optional

mixed rice with glazed root vegetables

You can vary the vegetables in this dish as you wish, and add other ingredients, such as cooked chestnuts, which are lovely in winter, or chickpeas (garbanzos), in place of some or all of the pine nuts.

serves 4

75g/3oz/scant $^1/_2$ cup brown rice
75g/3oz/scant $^1/_2$ cup wild rice
350ml/12fl oz/1$^1/_2$ cups water
salt
freshly ground black pepper
75g/3oz/scant $^1/_2$ cup basmati rice

for the glazed root vegetables:
1kg/2lb/6$^1/_2$ cups mixed root vegetables, such as parsnips, carrots, turnips and swedes (rutabagas), peeled or scraped and cut into even-sized pieces
50g/2oz/5tbsp pine nuts
40g/1$^1/_2$oz/generous 2tbsp vegan margarine

Put the brown rice and the wild rice into a saucepan with the water and $^1/_2$ teaspoon salt and bring to the boil. Cover, then turn the heat down and cook gently for 40 minutes, until both types of rice are tender and all the water has been absorbed.

Meanwhile, bring plenty of water to the boil in a medium-sized saucepan. Rinse the basmati rice in a sieve (strainer) under cold running water until the water runs clear. Add the rice to the boiling water and cook for about 10 minutes, or until tender. Drain.

Meanwhile, bring half a saucepan of water to the boil, then add the vegetables and cook for about 10 minutes, or until just tender. Drain.

Toast the pine nuts under a grill (broiler) – take care as they only take a few seconds to toast and burn easily.

To glaze the root vegetables, melt the margarine in a large saucepan with the olive oil. Add the lemon zest and juice, then the drained vegetables. Cook for about 10 minutes, stirring often, or until glazed and golden-brown in parts. Season with salt and pepper and stir in the parsley and toasted pine nuts.

Mix the basmati rice with the other two types of rice, fluff -up with a fork and check the seasoning. Make a "nest" of rice on a large serving dish or 4 individual plates and pile the vegetables in the centre. Spoon any remaining glaze in the pan over the vegetables.

1tbsp olive oil
grated zest and juice of 1 lemon
2–3tbsp roughly chopped fresh flat-leaf parsley

wild rice and chestnuts

Serve this rice dish with Cranberry Sauce (page 43), lightly cooked Brussels sprouts and some crisp roast potatoes or potato pancakes for an easy meal that has a festive flavour.

serves 4

10g/^{1}/4oz dried porcini mushrooms, optional
900ml/1^1/2 pints/3^3/4 cups boiling water
1tbsp oil
1 large onion, sliced
2 cloves garlic, crushed (minced)
2 celery sticks, sliced
175g/6oz/scant cup brown rice
50g/2oz/generous ^{1}/4 cup wild rice
125g/4oz/^{3}/4 cup dried chestnuts
a squeeze of lemon juice
salt
freshly ground black pepper
chopped fresh parsley, to garnish, optional

Put the porcini, if using, into a measuring jug and add the boiling water. Set aside to soak.

Heat the oil in a large saucepan or pressure cooker. Sauté the onion for 5 minutes, then add the garlic and celery and cook for a further 5 minutes.

Wash the brown rice, wild rice and chestnuts together in a sieve (strainer), then add to the onion mixture. Add the strained mushroom soaking liquor. Roughly chop the porcini and add to the pan.

Bring to the boil, cover, and either cook under pressure for 20 minutes or simmer gently for about 1 hour, until all the water has been absorbed and the chestnuts are tender.

Season with lemon juice, salt and pepper and top with a little chopped parsley, if using, before serving.

couscous with chickpea (garbanzo) stew

This spicy dish offers a delicious combination of flavours and textures *and* it's packed with nutrients. While it is generally served warm, it's also surprisingly good cold.

serves 3–4

If using dried beans, soak and cook them as described on page 97, then drain.

Heat 2 tablespoons of the oil. Add the onion, cover, and cook gently for 10 minutes, until tender. Add the carrots, cover, and cook for 4–5 minutes, then stir in the cinnamon, cumin and coriander and cook for a minute longer.

Add the tomato purée (paste), tomatoes, chickpeas (garbanzos), raisins or apricots and half the water. Bring to the boil, cover, and cook gently for about 25 minutes, or until the carrots are very tender and the liquid has thickened and reduced. Season to taste.

Meanwhile, prepare the couscous. Put the remaining water into a saucepan with a little salt, if you wish, and the remaining olive oil and bring to the boil. Pour in the couscous, stir, then cover and leave to cook over a very gentle heat for 4–5 minutes, until the couscous has absorbed all the water. Stir gently with a fork to break it up.

Put the couscous on a large platter or individual plates and the chickpea (garbanzo) mixture in the centre. Sprinkle the coriander (cilantro), if using, over the chickpea (garbanzo) mixture.

3tbsp olive oil

1 large onion, chopped

2 carrots, peeled and cut into 6mm/^{1}/$_{4}$in dice

1tsp ground cinnamon

1tsp ground cumin

1tsp ground coriander

2tbsp tomato purée (paste)

2 tomatoes, chopped

425g/15oz can chickpeas (garbanzos), drained, or 100g/3^{1}/$_{2}$oz/^{1}/$_{2}$ cup dried chickpeas (garbanzos)

75g/3oz/^{1}/$_{2}$ cup raisins or chopped dried apricots

900ml/1^{1}/$_{2}$ pints/3^{3}/$_{4}$ cups water

350g/12oz/2 cups couscous

salt

freshly ground black pepper

2tbsp chopped fresh coriander (cilantro), to garnish, optional

tabbouleh

This Middle Eastern salad can be made with either bulgur wheat or couscous – either way it's a delicious hot weather salad with a light, refreshing flavour. It needs to be made well in advance – 12 hours is the minimum, and 48 hours is fine – to allow the flavours to infuse.

serves 4

250g/8oz/1^1/3 cups couscous or bulgur wheat, unsoaked

4 large tomatoes, diced

^{1}/2 cucumber, diced

4tbsp lemon juice

1 clove garlic, crushed (minced)

8tbsp chopped fresh parsley

4tbsp chopped fresh mint

salt

freshly ground black pepper

lemon slices, tomato slices and black olives, optional, to garnish

Put the unsoaked couscous or bulgur wheat into a large bowl. Add the tomatoes and cucumber to the couscous or bulgur wheat, together with the lemon juice, garlic, parsley and mint. Stir well and season with salt and pepper. Cover and refrigerate for 48 hours, then taste and add more salt and pepper, if necessary.

Spoon the mixture into a shallow serving dish. Garnish with lemon, tomato and black olives, if using. Alternatively, press the mixture into a 2–2.5 litre/3^1/2–4 pint ring mould (tube pan). Press down firmly, then refrigerate until needed. When you want to serve the dish, turn it out and fill the centre with watercress, black olives or sliced tomatoes.

rice salad with oyster mushrooms and avocado

serves 4

Half fill a large saucepan with water and bring to the boil. Add the rice and cook for about 45 minutes, or until tender, then drain.

Meanwhile, heat the olive oil in a saucepan and fry the oyster mushrooms and garlic for about 4 minutes, or until the mushrooms are tender. Season with salt and pepper. Toss the avocado in the lemon juice and season to taste.

Combine the rice, oyster mushrooms, avocado, pine nuts, spring onions (scallions) or chives and parsley and serve warm or cold.

225g/8oz/generous cup
brown rice
2tbsp olive oil
225g/8oz/2^{2}/3 cups oyster
mushrooms
2 cloves garlic, crushed
(minced)
salt
freshly ground black pepper
1 ripe avocado, stoned
(pitted), peeled and sliced
juice of 1 lemon
50g/2oz/scant ^{1}/2 cup pine
nuts, toasted
2–3tbsp chopped spring
onions (scallions)
or chives
a little fresh flat-leaf
parsley, torn

creamy nut korma

In this delicately spiced dish, ground almonds are used with coconut cream to thicken the sauce, to which lightly cooked vegetables are added. It's good with plain basmati rice, a tomato salsa and Indian bread – naan, poppadums or chapattis.

serves 4

2tbsp oil
1 onion, chopped
2 cloves garlic, crushed (minced)
2.5cm/1in piece of fresh root ginger, grated (minced)
8–10 cardamom pods, crushed
1/2tsp turmeric
1tsp ground cumin
1tsp ground coriander
50g/2oz/1/4 cup creamed coconut, thinly sliced
400ml/15fl oz/scant 2 cups water
100g/31/2oz/generous cup ground almonds
1–2tbsp freshly squeezed lemon juice
salt
freshly ground black pepper

Heat the oil in a large saucepan. Add the onion, cover, and fry over a gentle heat for 7 minutes, then add the garlic. Add the ginger and cardamom to the pan, with the turmeric, cumin and ground coriander. Stir and leave to cook gently for 1 minute – take care not to burn the spices.

Add the coconut to the pan with the water and bring to the boil. Stir, then leave to melt completely. Add the ground almonds to the pan and cook for a moment or two. Purée the mixture in a food processor or blender or leave it as is.

Add the lemon juice, salt and pepper to taste. Set aside while the vegetables are prepared.

Half fill a large saucepan with water and bring to the boil. Add the vegetables and cook for 3–4 minutes, or until just tender. Drain the vegetables, then return them to the pan and add the creamy spice mixture. Check the seasoning and reheat gently. Sprinkle with the coriander (cilantro), if using, and serve.

450g/1lb/4 cups cauliflower florets

200g/7oz/generous 2 cups fine green beans, trimmed and halved

200g/7oz/1^{1}/2 cups carrots, scraped and thinly sliced

2–4tbsp chopped fresh coriander (cilantro), to garnish, optional

stuffed nut roast

Nut roasts can be delicious. This festive favourite goes well with all the traditional Christmas accompaniments – Cranberry Sauce, Vegan Gravy, Bread Sauce (pages 44, 45 and 43) as well as crisp roast potatoes and seasonal vegetables.

serves 8–12

2tbsp olive oil

2 large onions, finely chopped

4tbsp plain (all-purpose) flour

300ml/10fl oz/1$\frac{1}{4}$ cups water

225g/8oz/1$\frac{1}{2}$ cups cashew nuts, finely grated

225g/8oz/1$\frac{1}{2}$ cups blanched almonds, finely grated

225g/8oz/4 cups fresh white breadcrumbs

4tbsp lemon juice

salt

freshly ground black pepper

freshly grated nutmeg

Preheat the oven to 190°C/375°F/Gas 5. Grease a 900g/2lb loaf tin (loaf pan) and line the base and ends with greased non-stick baking parchment.

Heat the oil in a large saucepan. Add the onion and fry gently, covered, for about 10 minutes, or until tender. Stir occasionally and do not let the onion brown.

Add the flour to the onion, stir for a moment over the heat, then pour in the water and stir until thickened. Remove from the heat and add the nuts, breadcrumbs, lemon juice and salt, pepper and grated nutmeg. Set aside.

To make the stuffing, put the breadcrumbs into a bowl and add the rest of the ingredients, and a little salt and pepper. Mix with a fork until combined, then form into a flat rectangle the size of the loaf tin (loaf pan).

Spoon half the nut mixture into the prepared loaf tin (loaf pan), smooth the surface level, then place the rectangle of stuffing on top. Cover with the remaining nut mixture, smooth the top with the back of a spoon. Bake for 1 hour, or until firm in the middle and lightly browned on top.

When the nut roast is ready, remove it from the oven and leave to stand for 4–5 minutes, then slip a knife round the sides to loosen. Place a warmed serving plate on top, and turn out the nut roast. Garnish with the parsley and lemon slices, if using.

for the stuffing:
175g/6oz/3 cups fresh white breadcrumbs
4tbsp olive oil
1 small onion, grated
grated zest of 1 unwaxed lemon
1tsp mixed herbs
large handful of fresh parsley, chopped, plus sprigs of parsley, to garnish
lemon slices, to garnish, optional

polenta

Polenta – finely milled corn – can be made into a kind of porridge, served straight from the pan, or it can be pressed flat, allowed to cool, then grilled (broiled), baked or fried until golden. Here it's served with a Fresh Tomato Sauce (page 47), but it is good with any tasty sauce or the Mustard Cream Dressing (page 31).

serves 4

250g/8oz/1^1/3 cups polenta
1 litre/1^3/4 pints/4 cups water
salt
freshly ground black pepper
olive oil, for frying

to serve:
1 quantity Fresh Tomato Sauce (page 47)
lemon wedges, to garnish

Put the polenta into a medium-sized saucepan and mix to a smooth paste with the water. Cook over a medium heat, stirring gently and continuously, until the mixture comes to the boil and becomes thick and smooth. Continue to cook gently for 30 minutes, until the polenta is very thick and comes away from the sides of the pan. Season with plenty of salt and pepper.

Using a palette knife, spread the polenta on a flat plate, baking sheet or tray until about 1cm (^{1}/2in) thick, then leave it to cool completely.

Just before you want to serve the polenta, cut it into slices. Fry the slices in a little hot olive oil in a frying pan until crisp on both sides; drain on kitchen paper.

Alternatively, brush the polenta slices on both sides with olive oil, then place under a hot grill (broiler) and cook on both sides until golden. Another option is to brush the polenta slices with oil as before and place on a baking sheet and bake near the top of an oven preheated to 200°C/400°F/Gas 6 for 30–40 minutes, turning them after about 20 minutes.

Serve with the Fresh Tomato Sauce, garnished with lemon wedges.

Once you start to plan meals around complex carbohydrates, like potatoes, pasta and grains, you realize how versatile these ingredients are. A whole range of exciting dishes opens up, and these foods really come into their own.

This is especially true of potatoes, which for years have been very much in the second division and accused of making us fat. There are numerous excellent potato dishes – here you will find just a taste of the many possibilities, which I hope you'll enjoy.

baked potatoes with vegan toppings

Prepare baked potatoes in the usual way. Scrub 1 large, old potato per person, prick it several times with a fork, or cut a cross on the top. Bake in a preheated 230°C/450°F/Gas 8 oven for about 1 hour or in a microwave on full power for 4–5 minutes for each potato, until tender.

Serve baked potatoes with a knob of vegan margarine and/or any of the following fillings:

- cooked, drained sweetcorn
- chopped fresh herbs
- cooked, drained red kidney beans
- shredded lettuce and chopped tomato
- Hummus (page 13)
- Tahini Dip (page 14)
- Guacamole (page 15)
- Tapenade (page 16)
- Sweet Red Pepper and Garlic Dip (page 17)
- Tofu and Sun-dried Tomato Dip (page 18)
- Tofu, Cashew and Fresh Herb Dip (page 18)
- Fresh Tomato Sauce (page 47)
- Béchamel Sauce (page 49)
- Tomato Salsa (page 51)
- Confit of Red Onions (page 54)
- Homemade Coleslaw (page 33)
- Vegan Mayonnaise (page 30)
- Mustard Cream Dressing (page 31).

quick potato pancakes

These are the simplest potato pancakes to make, but are equally delicious.

serves 2

Mix the grated potatoes (do not be tempted to rinse them, because the starch is necessary to hold the pancakes together) with a sprinkling of salt to taste. Heat the oil in a frying pan and add spoonfuls of the potato mixture, flattening them with the back of the spoon. Fry them for about 3 minutes on each side, until golden and crisp. Drain the pancakes on kitchen paper, then serve immediately.

2 large potatoes, about 500g/1lb 2 oz/3^{1}/$_2$ cups, peeled and coarsely grated
salt
4tbsp olive oil

healthy chips (fries)

Chips needn't be bad for you. If baked in a little oil and served with a large green salad and some grated carrot, you need never feel guilty about eating chips (fries) again.

serves 4

350g/12oz/2¹/₂ cups potatoes, scrubbed or peeled and cut into thick chips (fries)

1tsp olive oil

Preheat the oven to 230°C/450°F/Gas 8. Place a non-stick baking sheet or large roasting tin in the oven. Rinse the potatoes under cold running water, drain and pat dry. Drizzle the oil over the chips (fries), turning them with your hands until they are coated in the oil.

Put the chips (fries) on the heated baking sheet or in the tin in a single layer. Bake for about 40 minutes, turning them occasionally, until they are golden brown and crisp all over. Serve immediately.

golden spiced potato

Serve this with a Tomato, Black Olive and Red Onion Salad (page 35) and perhaps a steamed vegetable, such as fine green beans, or a green salad. The mixture also makes a good stuffing for tomatoes, the instructions for which are given below.

serves 4

Heat the oil in a medium-sized saucepan. Add the onion and fry for 8 minutes, then add the garlic, turmeric, ground coriander and cumin seeds.

Add the potatoes, turning them gently with a spoon until they become coated with the onion and spice mixture, then add the water and season with salt and pepper. Cover and leave to cook gently for about 10 minutes, until the potatoes are just tender. Shake the pan from time to time to prevent the potatoes sticking and ensure even cooking.

Check the seasoning, adjusting if necessary, then serve, sprinkled with the parsley or coriander (cilantro), if using.

2tbsp oil
1 onion, chopped
1 clove garlic, crushed
(minced)
1/2tsp turmeric
1tsp ground coriander
1tsp cumin seeds
900g/2lb/6 cups potatoes,
peeled and cut into 1cm/
1/2in cubes
150ml/5fl oz/generous 1/2
cup water
salt
freshly ground black pepper
1–2tbsp chopped fresh
coriander (cilantro) or
parsley, to garnish, optional

variation

tomatoes stuffed with golden spiced potato

Choose large, firm tomatoes, slice off the tops, scoop out the seeds, and fill with the cooked potato mixture. Stand the tomatoes in a shallow baking dish and bake at 180°C/350°F/Gas 4 for 15–20 minutes, until the tomatoes have heated through. Serve with a lightly cooked green vegetable, such as fresh spinach, or a crisp green salad, and with some brown rice if you want a more substantial meal.

spiced spinach and potatoes

I love the combination of potatoes and dark green leafy vegetables. I'm not alone as it is found in a number of peasant dishes around the world. From Ireland, there's the soothing Colcannon (page 140), while India offers this spicy mixture, which is very different in character, yet equally appealing. It's good with Dal (page 101), or otherwise served simply with plain rice or Indian breads and, perhaps, a simple tomato salad or raita, spicy pickles or chutney.

serves 2

2tbsp oil

1 red chilli, fresh or dried

2tsp cumin seeds

$^{1}/_{2}$tsp turmeric

1 onion, chopped

1 clove garlic, crushed (minced)

225g/8oz/1$^{1}/_{2}$ cups potatoes, peeled and cut into 1cm/$^{1}/_{2}$in cubes

500g/1lb 2oz/9 cups fresh spinach, trimmed, or frozen leaf spinach

salt

freshly ground black pepper

Heat the oil in a large saucepan, then add the whole chilli, the cumin seeds and turmeric. Stir over the heat for a few seconds, letting the spices fry but not burn – watch them because they catch easily.

Add the onion, garlic and potatoes, stir, cover, and leave to cook gently for about 15 minutes, or until the potatoes are tender. Stir from time to time and add a little water if the vegetables start to stick.

Meanwhile, prepare and cook the spinach. If using fresh spinach, wash it and put the leaves, still damp, into a large saucepan without any extra water. Cover and cook for 5–8 minutes, until tender. If using frozen spinach, cook it in 6mm/$^{1}/_{4}$in of boiling water for about 3 minutes, until tender. Drain the spinach.

Remove the chilli from the potato mixture, then add the spinach. Season with salt and pepper and serve.

provençal potatoes

This is good served with a green salad or lightly cooked green beans, cabbage or spinach.

serves 2

Heat the oil in a medium-sized saucepan for 5 minutes. Add the onion and fry until it begins to soften. Add the garlic and tomatoes, breaking the tomatoes up roughly with a spoon. Bring to the boil and let the mixture simmer for 10–15 minutes, until it is very thick and the excess liquid has evaporated.

Meanwhile, bring 5cm/2in of water to the boil in a large pan. Add the potatoes, cover, and simmer for 7–10 minutes, until tender but not breaking up, then drain.

Add the sun-dried tomatoes to the tomato sauce, along with the olives. Season with salt and black pepper. Add the potatoes to the sauce, then serve immediately.

1tbsp olive oil
1 onion, chopped
1 clove garlic, crushed
(minced)
425g/15oz can tomatoes
350g/12oz/2^{1}/2 cups
potatoes, peeled and cut
into 5mm/^{1}/4in thick slices
2 sun-dried tomatoes in oil,
drained, chopped
50g/2oz/^{2}/3 cup black olives
salt
freshly ground black pepper

colcannon

This traditional Irish dish – and the simpler variation, Champ (given below) – shows just how good and nutritious simple, cheap ingredients can be. Colcannon can be a way of getting reluctant children (or adults) to eat more dark green leafy vegetables – it's certainly one of the best ways to cook kale. Extra-virgin olive oil isn't traditionally Irish, of course, but I prefer it to margarine, although I give the quantity for margarine if you would like to try it and decide which you like best.

serves 4

750g/1^1/2lb/4^1/2 cups potatoes, peeled and cut into even-sized pieces
750g/1^1/2lb/7 cups kale or dark cabbage, tough stems and leaves removed, and shredded
2 leeks, washed and finely sliced
125ml/4fl oz/^{1}/2 cup soya milk or soya cream
salt
freshly ground black pepper
4tbsp extra-virgin olive oil or 50g/2oz/4tbsp vegan margarine

Put the potatoes into a pan and cover with boiling water. Cover and simmer for 15–20 minutes, until they are tender.

Meanwhile, put about 1cm (^{1}/2in) of water into another pan and bring to the boil. Add the kale or cabbage, cover, and cook for 15–20 minutes (it needs to be cooked longer than usual for this recipe).

Put the leeks into a saucepan with the milk or cream and simmer gently for about 5–6 minutes, until tender. Put the oil or margarine into a small bowl and place this on top of the pan containing the leeks and milk until warmed through.

Drain the kale or cabbage and chop it, then return it to the pan to keep warm.

Drain the potatoes and mash them with the leeks and milk or cream. Add the kale, mix and season well with salt and pepper. Make sure the mixture is very hot, then transfer it to a warmed serving dish or plates. Make a well in the centre and pour the warmed oil or melted margarine into it.

variation

champ

For this version, which is simpler but equally good, leave out the kale or cabbage. Boil and drain the potatoes as described, then mash with the leeks and soya milk or cream and top with the warmed oil or melted margarine, as above.

rosti with spring onions (scallions)

Rosti is very quick and simple to make. You can vary it by adding different ingredients, such as fresh or dried herbs, onion, grated (minced) fresh root ginger and spices. This version is good served with a juicy salad like tomato and basil.

serves 2

500g/1lb/3 cups potatoes, scrubbed
small bunch of spring onions (scallions), chopped
salt
4tbsp oil

Put the potatoes into a saucepan, cover with cold water and bring to the boil. Boil for about 5 minutes, or until they are just tender on the outside. Drain the potatoes and leave until cool enough to handle, then remove the skins.

Grate the potatoes coarsely, mix in the spring onions (scallions) and season with a little salt.

Heat the oil in a frying pan, then add the potatoes and press down with a spatula, to make one large round. Fry the rosti over a moderate heat for about 7 minutes, until it is crisp and brown on the bottom.

Turn the rosti by turning it out on to a plate, then sliding it back into the frying pan. Continue to cook the rosti until brown and crisp on both sides, then drain on kitchen paper. Sprinkle with salt and serve at once.

spiced vegetables

This is very easy to make and good served on its own or with a Tomato, Black Olive and Red Onion Salad (page 35) or boiled brown rice, or as part of a number of spicy dishes when feeding a crowd. This dish tastes even better made a day in advance and reheated when needed. In fact, it can stand several reheatings and tastes better each time.

serves 4–6

Heat the oil in a pan. Add the spices, garlic, ginger and chilli and fry for 1–2 minutes. Add the onions and fry gently for 5 minutes.

Add the rest of the vegetables, turning them gently in the spicy mixture until they become coated.

Add the water, bring to the boil, cover, and cook gently for about 15 minutes, or until the vegetables are just tender and most of the liquid has been absorbed. Season with salt and pepper and garnish with fresh, chopped coriander (cilantro).

4tbsp olive oil
1tsp white mustard seeds
4tsp turmeric
2tbsp ground coriander
14–16 curry leaves or $^1/_2$tsp curry powder
4 cloves garlic, crushed
4cm/1$^1/_2$in piece of fresh root ginger, grated (minced)
1 green chilli, deseeded and chopped
2 onions, chopped
700g/1$^1/_2$lb/4$^1/_2$ cups potatoes, diced
1 large cauliflower, divided into florets
125g/4oz/generous cup green beans
2 large carrots, sliced
8 spinach or cabbage leaves, roughly shredded
200ml/7fl oz/scant cup water

desserts

Vegan desserts are a delight for there are almost endless options and these recipes give you a taste of some of them.

I've started with the useful Vegan Cream, which is very versatile and makes a change from the soya cream you can buy. Then there's a selection of cold and hot desserts. I am particularly delighted with the vegan version of that delicious Indian ice-cream, Kulfi, Instant Vegan Raspberry Ice, Chocolate Mousse, Chocolate Torte, Boozy Vegan Christmas Pudding Ice cream (as you will gather, I love ice cream and chocolate) and the Steamed Syrup Pudding (Dessert) – a wonderful treat for a cold winter's day.

Look out, too, for some of the vegan desserts you can buy, and don't forget, of course, fresh fruit, simply served as it is or made into a fruit salad or compote. There are now many vegan yogurts, vegan ice-creams and sorbets to buy but do read the ingredients on the labels first. Try nuts and dried fruits as they make delicious desserts – fresh dates are a particularly favourite.

Alternatively, you could take the savoury route and finish a meal with savoury crackers or oatcakes with or without a tangy dip like Tofu, Cashew and Fresh Herb (page 18), in lieu of cheese.

vegan cream

serves 4–6

In a small bowl, blend the cornflour (cornstarch) with a little of the soya milk to make a paste.

Put the rest of the milk into a saucepan with the vanilla pod (bean) and bring to the boil, then pour it into the cornflour (cornstarch) mixture, stir, and return to the pan. Stir over the heat for a minute or two until the mixture thickens, then remove from the heat and leave to cool. When cool, remove the vanilla pod (bean), rinse, dry and keep to use it again.

In another bowl, beat the margarine until it is light and creamy, then gradually whisk in the cooled cornflour (cornstarch) mixture. It is important to add the cornflour (cornstarch) mixture gradually, whisking well, to produce a beautifully light whipped cream.

Add the icing sugar (confectioner's sugar) towards the end, a teaspoonful at a time, tasting the mixture after each addition until it tastes sweet enough.

The delicate vanilla flavour can be enhanced with a drop or two of vanilla extract, if you wish, or you can add a splash of brandy or rum or orange flower or rose water, depending on what you are serving it with.

1tsp cornflour (cornstarch)
150ml/5fl oz/generous $\frac{1}{2}$ cup unsweetened soya milk
1 vanilla pod (bean)
100g/3$\frac{1}{2}$oz/scant $\frac{1}{2}$ cup vegan margarine
2–3tsp icing (confectioner's) sugar
a few drops of vanilla extract, brandy, rum, orange flower or rose water, optional

pears in red wine

These are good served just as they are or with a spoonful of Vegan Cream (page 145), soya cream or a refreshing sorbet.

serves 4

50g/2oz/generous $\frac{1}{4}$ cup sugar

300ml/10fl oz/1$\frac{1}{4}$ cups red wine

grated zest of 1 well-scrubbed orange

300ml/10fl oz/1$\frac{1}{4}$ cups water

4 firm dessert pears, peeled, retaining the stalks

1tbsp finely chopped preserved ginger in syrup

Put the sugar into a saucepan with the wine, orange zest and water and heat gently until the sugar has dissolved, then bring to the boil.

Add the pears, cover, and simmer gently for 30–40 minutes, or until the pears are tender right through. Don't undercook them or the insides will turn brown.

Remove the pears from the pan with a slotted spoon and place them in a serving dish.

Add the ginger to the poaching liquor in the pan and boil vigorously until it has reduced and looks shiny and syrupy, then pour this over the pears. Leave to cool. Serve at room temperature or chilled.

peaches in wine

A simple but very good fruit dish.

serves 4

To skin the peaches, put them into a deep bowl. Cover with boiling water and leave for 2–3 minutes, until the skins can be removed easily with the point of a knife.

Slice the peaches, removing the stones (pits). Put the slices into a glass bowl, or individual serving dishes, and sprinkle with the sugar.

Pour the wine over the peaches, then chill for at least 30 minutes, or until needed.

4 large, ripe peaches
1 rounded tbsp caster (granulated) sugar
120ml/4fl oz/$^1/_2$ cup sweet white wine

instant vegan raspberry ice

With a packet of frozen raspberries in the freezer and a couple of packets of soya cream in the cupboard, you can always whizz up a dessert at the last minute.

serves 6

450g/1lb/1³/₄ cups frozen raspberries, straight from the freezer
125g/4oz/generous ¹/₂ cup caster (granulated) sugar
2 × 250ml/8fl oz packets soya cream

Place all the ingredients in a food processor and whizz until thick and creamy. Serve at once. Any leftovers will keep for an hour or so in the freezer, but it is best served fresh.

kulfi

This is a fabulous "cheats'"version of this sweet, aromatic Indian ice-cream. It's absolutely delicious.

Pour the soya cream into a saucepan. Crush the cardamom pods with a pestle and mortar or in a bowl with a wooden spoon and add to the soya cream. Bring to the boil, then remove from the heat, cover, and leave for 30 minutes to allow the flavours to infuse.

Add the sugar, reheat and stir over a low heat for a minute or two, until the sugar has dissolved, then remove from the heat. Strain the mixture into a polythene container and stir in half the nuts.

Leave to cool, then freeze, stirring from time to time as it becomes frozen around the edges.

Remove from the freezer 15–20 minutes before serving, then scoop into bowls and top with the remaining pistachios.

2 × 250ml/8fl oz packets soya cream
8 cardamom pods
150g/5oz/^{3}/$_4$ cup caster (granulated) sugar
50g/2oz/^{1}/$_2$ cup shelled pistachio nuts, finely chopped

boozy vegan christmas pudding ice-cream

This makes a wonderful frozen Christmas pudding (plum pudding) if you freeze it in a plastic mixing bowl, but it's also good served in scoops at any time of the year.

serves 6–8

1tbsp cornflour (cornstarch)
900ml/1^1/2 pints/3^3/4 cups soya milk
1 vanilla pod (bean)
2tbsp sugar
50g/2oz/^{1}/4 cup vegan margarine
100g/4oz/^{2}/3 cup vegan plain (bittersweet) chocolate, broken into pieces
125g/4oz/^{2}/3 cup glacé (candied) cherries
50g/2oz/^{1}/3 cup whole (candied) mixed peel
50g/2oz/scant ^{1}/2 cup (golden seedless) raisins or sultanas
4tbsp rum or brandy
25g/1oz/^{1}/3 cup flaked (slivered) almonds

Put the cornflour (cornstarch) in a bowl with a little of the milk to make a paste.

Put the rest of the milk into a saucepan with the vanilla pod (bean), sugar, margarine and chocolate. Heat gently to boiling point, then pour the mixture over the cornflour (cornstarch) and mix until combined. Return to the saucepan and bring to the boil, stirring. Remove from the heat, cover, and leave to cool.

Remove the vanilla pod (bean)and rinse, dry and reuse it another time. Liquidize the mixture, then pour it into a polythene container or pudding bowl and freeze until it is frozen around the edges. Whisk, and return to the freezer.

Repeat this process, whisking in the fruits and rum or brandy, then let the ice-cream freeze until solid.

Remove from the freezer an hour before serving, then beat it or, if you have frozen it in a pudding basin, simply turn it out, like a Christmas pudding.

rum-marinated fruits with coconut and lime cream

Combine the pineapple, bananas and papaya with half the lime juice, the sugar and rum. Cover and leave to marinate for at least 1 hour, stirring from time to time.

Meanwhile, make the coconut cream. Put the creamed coconut into a small saucepan with the sugar and boiling water. Stir until dissolved, heat gently, if necessary. Remove from the heat, stir in the lime juice and zest and leave to cool.

Serve the fruit with the coconut cream.

1 ripe pineapple, peeled, cored and diced
2 bananas, peeled and chopped
1 ripe papaya, peeled and sliced
grated zest and juice of 1 lime
50g/2oz/generous $^{1}/_{4}$ cup brown sugar
4tbsp dark rum

for the coconut cream:
100g/3$^{1}/_{2}$oz/scant $^{1}/_{2}$ cup creamed coconut, cut into pieces
1tbsp caster sugar (granulated sugar)
4tbsp boiling water
grated zest and juice of 1 lime

chocolate mousse

100g/3^1/2oz/generous ^{1}/2 cup vegan plain (bitter-sweet) chocolate, broken into pieces

250ml/8fl oz/1 cup soya cream, plus extra, as required, to serve

1tbsp brandy, rum, Amaretto or Cointreau

a few toasted flaked (slivered) almonds, to decorate, optional

Put the chocolate into a bowl, placed over a pan of gently simmering water – the bottom of the bowl should be above the surface of the water – and leave for a few minutes, until the chocolate has melted.

Add the soya cream and alcohol to the chocolate, then whisk until the mixture has cooled and thickened a little.

Pour the mousse into 4 serving dishes and chill overnight, until it is lightly set. Top each serving with a spoon of soya cream and a few toasted almonds, if using.

chocolate torte

Although it's luxurious and impressive, this is actually very easy to make and great for a special occasion.

serves 8–10

Put the chocolate into a bowl, placed over a pan of gently simmering water – the bottom of the bowl should be above the surface of the water – and leave for a few minutes, until the chocolate has melted.

Meanwhile put the digestive biscuits (Graham crackers) into a polythene bag and crush with a rolling pin to make crumbs. Put these into a bowl and add the melted chocolate. Mix well, then press into the base of a 21cm (8½in) loose-bottomed cake tin (pan). Chill in the fridge while you make the top layer.

Put remaining chocolate into the bowl in which you melted the chocolate for the base and melt over simmering water as before. Add the soya cream and rum to the chocolate, then whisk thoroughly until the mixture has cooled and thickened a little. Pour on top of the base and smooth the top.

Cover the top of the tin with foil or a plate then chill for at least 3 hours. It must chill thoroughly – 12–24 hours is not too long – and make sure it is well covered so that it doesn't pick up any flavours from the fridge.

To serve, remove the sides of the tin (pan), leaving the Torte on the base, then slide it – still on its base for safety – onto a serving dish. Decorate with chocolate curls and/or sifted icing sugar (confectioner's sugar), if using.

for the base:
100g/3½oz/generous ½ cup vegan plain (bitter-sweet) chocolate, broken into pieces
175g/6oz/2 cups vegan digestive biscuits (Graham crackers)

for the top layer:
200g/7oz/generous cup vegan plain (bittersweet) chocolate, broken into pieces
2 × 125ml/4fl oz packets soya cream
1tbsp rum
chocolate curls and/or icing (confectioner's) sugar, to decorate, optional

rhubarb crumble (crisp)

This is easy to make because you don't need to cook the fruit first. It also makes a large quantity, but simply halve the amount to fill a smaller dish and serve less people.

serves 6–8

900g/2lb/8 cups rhubarb, cut into 2.5cm/1in pieces
75g/3oz/scant $^1/_2$ cup sugar

for the crumble topping:
250g/9oz/generous 2 cups wholewheat self-raising flour or half wholewheat, half white flour
175g/6oz/$^3/_4$ cup vegan margarine
175g/6oz/scant cup demerara (coarse light brown) sugar

Preheat the oven to 200°C/400°F/gas 6. Put the rhubarb into a lightly greased large, shallow heatproof dish. Mix in the sugar, then make sure that the fruit forms an even layer.

To make the crumble topping, put the flour into a mixing bowl and rub (cut) in the margarine with your fingertips until the mixture looks like fine breadcrumbs and there are no visible lumps of margarine. Add the sugar and mix gently.

Spoon the topping over the rhubarb, smoothing the top and ensuring the fruit is covered.

Bake in the preheated oven for 30–40 minutes, until the top is crisp and has browned lightly and the fruit feels tender when pierced with a skewer. Serve hot.

variations

plum crumble (crisp)

Use plums instead of rhubarb. Halve and stone (pit) the plums before putting them into the dish – unless you're using the very tiny damson plums, in which case just wash them and use whole. Finish with the crumble topping and bake as above.

blueberry crumble (crisp)

Blueberries make a lovely crumble (crisp). Simply replace the rhubarb with the same quantity of blueberries, rinse, and put them into the dish. Top with the crumble (crisp) mixture and bake as for the Rhubarb Crumble (Crisp).

blackcurrant pie

700g/1½lb/5 cups fresh or defrosted frozen blackcurrants, topped and tailed
150g/5oz/¾ cup soft brown or caster (granulated) sugar
1 quantity Basic Shortcrust Pastry (page 62)
soya milk, to glaze
caster (granulated) sugar , for sprinkling

First, put the blackcurrants into a heavy-based saucepan and cook gently for 4–5 minutes, until the juices start to run. Drain the fruit, removing the excess juice (which can be used for another dessert, such as jelly). Stir the sugar into the blackcurrants and set aside to cool.

Preheat the oven to 200°C/400°F/Gas 6 and grease a 24cm (9½in) pie plate.

On a lightly floured board, roll just over half the pastry into a round to fit the pie plate. Put the fruit into the pastry-lined plate to within 1cm (½in) of the edge. Dampen the edges with water.

Roll out the remaining pastry and place on top of the fruit. Press the edges together, trim, knock up (straighten) and flute (scallop) the edges with your fingers or press with a fork to seal and decorate them. Make a steam hole in the centre of the pastry. Cut decorations from the pastry trimmings, if you like, and attach these to the pie with water. Brush with soya milk, sprinkle caster sugar (granulated sugar) over the top and bake for 30 minutes. Serve hot or cold.

steamed syrup pudding (dessert)

This indulgent, old-fashioned dessert is wonderfully light, even though it is made without dairy products.

Fill a steamer with water and heat, or fill a saucepan with enough water to come half-way up a 900ml/1^{1}/2 pint pudding basin (mixing bowl) and bring to the boil.

Grease the basin (bowl) thoroughly with margarine, then put 2 tablespoons golden syrup (light corn syrup) into the bottom.

Cream the margarine with the 125g (4oz) golden syrup (light corn syrup) until light and fluffy. Mix in the flour.

Dissolve the bicarbonate of soda (baking soda) in the soya milk. Stir this mixture quickly into the margarine mixture and pour into the pudding basin (mixing bowl). Cover with a piece of greaseproof paper, pleated in the middle (so that it can expand as the mixture rises) and a piece of foil, also pleated. Tie securely under the rim of the basin with kitchen string.

Put the basin (bowl) into the steamer or saucepan, cover, and steam gently for 1^{1}/2 hours. Do not let the water go off the boil during this time, and keep an eye on the water level, topping it up, if necessary.

Turn the pudding (dessert) out of the basin (bowl) and serve with the extra syrup.

2tbsp golden (light corn) syrup, plus 125g/4oz/^{1}/3 cup, and extra, to serve

125g/4oz/^{1}/2 cup vegan margarine, plus extra for greasing

125g/4oz/1cup plain (all-purpose) flour, sifted

1tsp bicarbonate of (baking) soda

150ml/5fl oz/generous ^{1}/2 cup soya milk

christmas (plum) pudding

serves 8

225g/8oz/generous 1^1/$_2$
cups currants
125g/4oz/scant cup sultanas
(golden seedless raisins)
125g/4oz/scant cup raisins
125g/4oz/generous ^{1}/$_2$ cup
mixed (candied) peel,
chopped
25g/1oz/1tbsp blanched
almonds, chopped
125g/4oz/scant cup plain
(all-purpose) flour
^{1}/$_2$tsp salt
^{1}/$_2$tsp freshly grated nutmeg
^{1}/$_2$tsp ground ginger
1^1/$_2$tsp mixed spice
225g/8oz/generous cup
dark brown molasses (dark
brown) sugar
125g/4oz/2 cups soft, fresh,
wholewheat breadcrumbs
225g/8oz/2 cups pure
vegetable suet, grated
zest and juice of 1 lemon
1tbsp black treacle
100ml/4fl oz/^{1}/$_2$ cup soya
milk
4tbsp rum

Grease a 1.2 litre (2 pint) pudding basin (mixing bowl) or 2 x 600ml (1 pint) pudding basins (mixing bowls).

Put the dried fruit and almonds into a large bowl. Add the flour, salt, spices, sugar, breadcrumbs, suet, lemon zest and juice, treacle, soya milk and rum. Mix very well, to make a soft, dense mixture.

Spoon the mixture into the basin (bowl) or basins (bowls). Cover with a double layer of greased foil and tie down well under the rim.

Put into a steamer or a saucepan on top of an upturned saucer and pour in enough boiling water to come half-way up the sides of the basin (bowl). Steam for 4 hours, topping up the pan with boiling water as necessary. Leave to cool. Remove the foil and cut out a circle of greaseproof paper to fit over the top of the pudding, cover tightly with a fresh, doubled piece of foil, then store in a cool, dry place – the pudding or puddings will keep (and mature) for several months. To reheat, steam as before for 3 hours before serving.

I particularly enjoyed working on these recipes. Not because I am a great cake-eater, but because of the challenge of making cakes without eggs. In fact, what I found was that many cakes which were traditionally made with eggs can be adapted and made perfectly well without them. Our mothers and grandmothers also found this during the last war when they were forced to adapt recipes because eggs were unavailable. I hope you will enjoy my selection.

scones, cakes and cookies

scones

Home-made scones, eaten freshly baked, preferably still warm from the oven, are delicious, and are quick to make. Plain scones are nice with jam for tea, while flavoured ones make a good accompaniment to many savoury dishes and salads.

makes 8

225g/8oz/2 cups plain wholewheat (all-purpose) flour or half wholewheat and half white flour
2tsp baking powder
50g/ oz/^{1}/4 cup vegan margarine
150ml/5fl oz/generous ^{1}/2 cup soya milk or water

Preheat the oven to 220°C/425°F/Gas 7. Sift the flour and baking powder into a bowl, then add the margarine and rub it in with your fingertips until the mixture resembles fine breadcrumbs.

Add the milk or water gradually and mix to form a soft, but not sticky, dough. You may find that you need less milk or water or a little more than specified, depending on how absorbent your flour is, so add a small amount at a time until you have the right consistency.

Turn the dough out onto a floured board and knead lightly, then press out to a thickness of at least 1cm (^{1}/2in). Cut the scones out using a 5cm (2in) round cutter and place them on a floured baking sheet.

Bake in the preheated oven for 12–15 minutes, until the scones are golden brown and the sides spring back when lightly pressed. Cool on a wire rack or serve immediately.

variations

For sweet or savoury variations, add the following extras to the dry mixture before adding the milk or water, then finish as for the plain scones above.

basil and sun-dried tomato scones

Add 2 tablespoons roughly chopped or torn fresh basil and about 10 sun-dried tomatoes, drained and chopped.

onion and herb scones

Add a small to medium onion or a couple of shallots, finely chopped, and 2–3 teaspoons chopped fresh rosemary or thyme.

olive scones

Add 50–125g/2–4oz/scant to generous $\frac{1}{2}$ cup pitted black or green olives. You could add some chopped onion and crushed (minced) garlic, too, if you like.

garlic scones

Add 4–5 large garlic cloves, crushed (minced), mixing well to ensure they are distributed throughout the mixture.

sweet raisin scones

Add 50g/2oz/generous $\frac{1}{4}$ cup sugar and 50–100g/2–4oz/ scant $\frac{1}{2}$ to scant 1 cup raisins, plus $\frac{1}{2}$ teaspoon mixed spice or ground cinnamon for a sweet version.

fruit cake

This is based on a traditional farmhouse recipe, with vinegar and bicarbonate of soda (baking soda) used as the raising (rising) agents and no egg. It is light and moist, like a Dundee cake. It's best eaten fresh, but will keep for 7–10 days in an airtight tin.

makes one 20cm (8in) cake

350g/12oz/3 cups plain wholewheat (all-purpose) flour or half wholewheat and half white
1tsp mixed spice
175g/6oz/^{2}/3 cup vegan margarine
175g/6oz/scant cup real Barbados sugar
225g/8oz/generous 1^1/2 cups mixed dried fruit
125g/4oz/generous cup glacé (candied) cherries, rinsed, dried and halved, optional
grated zest of 1 well-scrubbed orange
2tbsp ground almonds
120ml/4fl oz/^{1}/2 cup soya milk
2tbsp red wine vinegar
^{3}/4tsp bicarbonate of (baking) soda

Preheat the oven to 150°C/300°F/Gas 2 and grease a 20cm (8in) cake tin (pan) and line with a double layer of greased greaseproof paper.

Sift the flour and mixed spice into a bowl, adding back the bran that remains in the sieve (sifter), if using wholewheat flour.

Rub the margarine into the flour with your fingers, until the mixture resembles fine breadcrumbs, then add the sugar, dried fruit, cherries, orange zest and ground almonds.

Warm half the soya milk in a small saucepan and add the vinegar. Dissolve the bicarbonate of (baking) soda in the rest of the soya milk, then add this to the milk and vinegar mixture. Stir this into the flour and fruit, mixing well until combined.

Spoon the mixture into the prepared cake tin (pan) and smooth the top. Bake in the preheated oven for 2–2^1/2 hours, until a skewer inserted into the centre of the cake comes out clean and the centre of the cake springs back a little when pressed.

Leave the cake in the tin (pan) to cool, then turn out and peel off the greaseproof paper.

variation

rich fruit cake

For a richer mixture, which makes a good Christmas or wedding cake, increase the amount of dried fruit to 500g/1lb 2oz/generous 3 cups and add 50g/2oz/^{2}/$_3$ cup flaked (slivered) almonds and 1 tablespoon black treacle. Add this mixture to the flour and margarine after they have been mixed together. Bake for the same length of time at the same temperature. When cool, prick the cake with a cocktail stick then pour 2 tablespoons of brandy over. Wrap in greaseproof paper and store in a tin until required. It will keep for 3–4 weeks, during which time you can "feed" it with another tablespoon or two of brandy. It can be covered in bought vegan marzipan and fondant icing, if desired.

sticky date ginger cake

This cake, which is similar to an old-fashioned gingerbread, becomes even more sticky and gooey if it's wrapped in greaseproof paper and stored in a tin for a week.

makes 12–16 slices

250g/8oz/2 cups plain wholewheat flour or half wholewheat and half white
2tsp ground ginger
1/2tsp bicarbonate of (baking) soda
125g/4oz/scant cup stoned (pitted) dates, chopped
50g/2oz/1/2 cup stem (candied) ginger in syrup, chopped
125g/4oz/generous 1/2 cup light soft brown sugar
150g/5oz/scant 1/2 cup black treacle
150g/5oz scant 1/2 cup golden (light corn) syrup
125ml/4fl oz/1/2 cup soya oil
125ml/4fl oz /1/2 cup soya milk

Preheat the oven to 150°C/300°F/Gas 2. Grease and line a 23cm (9in) square cake tin (pan) with non-stick baking parchment.

Sift the flour, ginger and bicarbonate of (baking) soda into a large bowl, adding any bran left in the sieve (sifter). Add the dates, syrup and sugar to the bowl.

Put the treacle and syrup into a saucepan and heat gently until melted, then remove from the heat and add the oil and milk, mixing well.

Add the treacle mixture to the bowl of dry ingredients, mix well, then pour the mixture into the prepared tin (pan). Bake for 50–60 minutes, or until a skewer inserted into the centre comes out clean. Leave to cool in the tin (pan) for 1 hour, then turn out onto a wire rack.

When the cake has cooled completely, wrap it in greaseproof paper and store in an airtight tin.

vegan sponge (layer) cake

This recipe makes an excellent light cake, very similar in texture to one made with eggs. The orange juice works with the raising (leavening) agent in the flour as well as the bicarbonate of (baking) soda and the soya flour to produce the light texture and attractive pale golden colour. You could intensify the orange by adding extra grated zest and orange icing (frosting) to make this a real orange cake or you could play it down by adding other flavourings, as suggested in the variations. Either way it works well, particularly with white flour, although wholewheat or a mixture of wholemeal and white also produce good results.

makes one 20–22cm (8–8¹/₂in) cake

Preheat the oven to 160°C/325°F/Gas 3. Grease 2 x 20–22cm (8–8¹/₂in) cake tins (pans) and line each with a circle of greased non-stick baking parchment.

Sift the flour, soya flour and bicarbonate of (baking) soda into a large bowl, adding back any bran left in the sieve (sifter). Add the sugar.

Into another bowl, add the oil, orange juice, water and vanilla extract. Whisk together to combine, then pour the mixture into the dry ingredients and mix well to a smooth, fairly wet batter.

Pour the mixture into the prepared cake tins (pans) and bake in the preheated oven for about 30 minutes, until the cakes start to shrink away from the sides of the tins (pans) and spring back when lightly pressed in the centre.

Leave the cakes to cool in the tins (pans) for 5 minutes, then turn out to cool on a wire rack. Peel off the paper and leave to cool completely.

Sandwich the cakes together with the jam and dust with icing (confectioner's) sugar.

275g/10oz/2¹/₂ cups self-raising (self-rising) white or wholewheat flour or half white, half wholewheat
50g/2oz/scant ¹/₂ cup soya flour
1tsp bicarbonate of (baking) soda
225g/8oz/generous cup caster (granulated) sugar
250ml/8fl oz/1 cup light olive oil
150ml/5fl oz/²/₃ cup orange juice
150ml/5fl oz/²/₃ cup cold water
1¹/₂tsp vanilla extract
3–4tbsp raspberry jam
icing (confectioner's) sugar, for dusting

variations

chocolate cake

Make as above, but replace 50g/2oz/scant $^{1}/_{2}$ cup of the flour with the same amount of (unsweetened) cocoa powder. To make the filling and icing (frosting), break 225g/8oz/1$^{1}/_{3}$ cups vegan plain (bittersweet) chocolate into pieces and melt in a bowl placed over a pan of simmering water. Stir in 4 tablespoons of soya milk. Sandwich the cakes together with half the chocolate mixture and coat the top with the rest. Decorate with grated chocolate.

orange cake

Add the grated zest of a well-scrubbed orange to the cake batter. For the icing (frosting) and filling, beat 125g/4oz/$^{1}/_{2}$ cup vegan margarine in a bowl until creamy, then sift in 200g/7oz/scant 1$^{1}/_{2}$ cups icing (confectioner's) sugar and beat again until light. Add 1 teaspoon of finely grated orange zest and 1–2 tablespoons orange juice, enough to loosen the mixture a little. Sandwich the cakes together with half the mixture and spread the remainder on top. Decorate with a few pieces of crystallized (candied) orange, flaked (slivered) almonds or whatever else you have to hand.

wholefood cake

Replace the white flour and white sugar with wholewheat flour and muscovado sugar (dark brown sugar). Sandwich the cake together with an all-fruit, no added sugar preserve and dust the top with ground almonds or a sprinkling of caster sugar (granulated sugar).

light ginger cake with lemon icing (frosting)

For this pleasant mixture of flavours, add 2 teaspoons of ground ginger and 50–125 g/2–4oz/generous $^{1}/_{4}$–generous $^{1}/_{2}$ cup preserved ginger in syrup, roughly chopped, to the basic sponge batter. Put the mixture into one deep 20–22cm (8–8$^{1}/_{2}$in) deep tin (pan), lined on the base and sides with non-stick baking parchment. Bake for about 1$^{1}/_{2}$ hours, until the top is firm and springs back when lightly pressed in the middle and a skewer inserted into the centre comes out clean. When it's cool, cover the top with an icing (frosting) made by sifting 125g/4oz/scant cup icing (confectioner's) sugar into a bowl, then gradually mixing in 1–2 tablespoons freshly squeezed lemon juice to make a stiff mixture. Scatter a few long, thin strips of lemon zest over the top (a zester is useful for this or use a knife).

chocolate cookie slices

These no-bake slices are easy to prepare but make sure that the cookies, margarine and chocolate you use do not contain any non-vegan ingredients.

makes 24

50g/2oz/¹/4 cup vegan margarine

50g/2oz/scant ¹/4 cup golden (light corn) syrup

200g/7oz/generous cup vegan plain (bittersweet) chocolate, broken into pieces

200g/7oz/1³/4 cups plain cookies

Line a Swiss roll tin (jelly roll pan) with non-stick baking parchment.

Put the margarine into a heavy-based, medium-sized saucepan with the syrup and half the chocolate. Heat gently until the chocolate has melted.

Meanwhile, crush the biscuits (cookies) with a rolling pin until you have coarse crumbs. Add the crumbs to the chocolate mixture and mix well until they are well coated.

Spoon the mixture into the tin (pan) and press down with the back of a spoon.

Melt the rest of the chocolate in a bowl, placed over a pan of simmering water (do not allow the bottom of the bowl to touch the water), and spread it over the top of the cookie mixture. Leave until cold and set, then cut into squares.

Jean's cookies

These wonderful, light, crumbly cookies are best when half-dipped in chocolate, although they're also good plain.

makes about 24

Preheat the oven to 140°C/275°F/Gas 1. Line a baking sheet with non-stick baking parchment.

Put the margarine and sugar into a bowl and beat until creamy. Beat in the remaining ingredients, to make a stiff dough.

Roll out the dough as thinly as you can on a lightly floured board. If you find it too crumbly to work, add a drop or two of water, but don't overdo it or the cookies will lose their crumbly texture.

Stamp out rounds with a cookie cutter and lift onto the prepared baking sheet – they'll hardly spread at all, so can be placed quite closely together. Bake in the preheated oven for 20 minutes.

Let the cookies cool on the tray until you can handle them, then, if you wish, dip each one in melted chocolate to half-coat it. Leave on a wire rack to finish cooling and let the chocolate set.

125g/4oz/$^1/_2$ cup vegan margarine
50g/2oz/generous $^1/_4$ cup caster (granulated) sugar
125g/4oz/$^2/_3$ cup porridge oats
25g/1oz/2tbsp plain (all-purpose) flour
25g/1oz/$^1/_4$ cup semolina
25g/1oz/$^1/_3$ cup desiccated (dried shredded) coconut
$^1/_2$tsp bicarbonate of (baking) soda
175–200g/6–8oz/1–1$^1/_3$ cups vegan plain (bitter-sweet) chocolate, melted, optional

classic flapjacks

These flapjacks are of the sticky, gooey type.

makes 16

175g/6 oz/³/₄ cup vegan margarine

175g/6oz/scant cup muscovado (dark brown) sugar

2tbsp golden (light corn) syrup

225g/8oz/1¹/₄ cups rolled oats – organic ones if possible

Preheat the oven to 190°C/375°F/Gas 5. Grease a Swiss roll tin (jelly roll pan) thoroughly with oil or margarine or line it with non-stick baking parchment.

Put the margarine, sugar and syrup into a medium-large saucepan and heat gently until melted. Remove from the heat and stir in the oats.

Spread the mixture out in the prepared tin (pan), smoothing it to the edges. Bake in the preheated oven for 20 minutes, until golden and crisp.

Leave to cool a little, then mark into slices. Leave in the tin (pan) until cold.

vegan macaroons

Crisp and crunchy, these are similar to traditional macaroons.

makes 12

Preheat the oven to 160°C/325°F/Gas 3. Cover a baking sheet with rice paper.

Put the semolina, ground almonds, caster (granulated) sugar and baking powder into a bowl and mix together. Add the almond essence and water and mix to a soft consistency.

Put spoonfuls of the mixture onto the rice paper, forming each one into a rough circle, leaving some room in between as they spread a little during cooking. Put a blanched almond on top of each cookie.

Bake in the preheated oven for about 25 minutes, until golden brown. Leave to cool and crisp on the baking sheet, then break off the excess rice paper.

50g/2oz/^{1}/$_2$ cup semolina
50g/2oz/^{2}/$_3$ cup ground almonds
75g/3oz/scant ^{1}/$_2$ cup golden caster (golden granulated) sugar
1tsp baking powder
^{1}/$_2$tsp almond essence
5tbsp water
12 blanched almonds
rice paper

index